Confessions
of an
Unemployed
Professional

The Survival Guide for Dealing with
Workplace Conflict, Unemployment Stress,
and How to Discover Your Passion

JARED C. POWELL

Books to Live By, Inc.

COPYRIGHT

Disclaimer and Legal Notices

ISBN 13: 978-1537155005

ISBN 10: 1537155008

ACKNOWLEDGMENTS

To my incredible parents for their unconditional love and for giving me life; to my amazing brother who has been an true inspiration all my life, and one whom I want to say thank you to, I am so proud to call you my best friend; to my unbelievable sister who continually baffles me at what an amazing woman she has become; to my new fantastic siblings, treasured family, and friends, thank you for your patience, generosity, support, and encouragement.

This endeavor has been one of the biggest challenges of my life, but the work has been an absolute labor of love. I write this book in honor of all the individuals who want to live his or her dreams and follow their passion.

CONTENTS

Preface

The day was July 23rd; I distinctly remember this date because I was stuck in a monthly workstream meeting I scheduled at the local Hilton Hotel. The room was filled with over 20 company men and women from various departments of a large healthcare organization—we will call it Lexington International. I was the senior project manager driving the meeting and was ultimately responsible for the success of the project.

After I presented my contribution on the agenda, I was complimented on my delivery and presentation skills. Immediately, the questions came pouring in, which I deflected to my project team since they were the subject matter experts. Though, as the questions became more and more convoluted, I sat there trying to mask my frustration, as well as confusion, to maintain the illusion that I was following the conversation perfectly. Seconds later, the thoughts crept in, "Is this as good as it gets? Is this work part of what I really want to do with my life? Is my purpose really to discuss the joys of locum tenens for 3 hours?"

I always thought I'd write a book, own a franchise, write a song, or even work at a tech start-up and create the next big mobile app. I knew I wanted to do something creative and inventive, something in which I could use more of my imagination, but I didn't want to go backward and work at some $11-an- hour job to "pay my dues" all over again. All I knew for certain was I wanted more out of life, since I was not happy living the life I was living.

This was me in 2011—I was so miserable! I eventually decided to leave my position to set out to discover new paths and somehow follow my dreams. Since then, I have explored new passions, made new friends, collected new skills, and made more money than I ever thought possible, all the while making a host of costly mistakes and hard choices.

This book describes my eye-opening moments and offers tips for handling financial issues, along with techniques for finding a job that fits your personality and style. In this book you will also find strategies for coping with workplace dysfunction, depression, guilt, and methods of overcoming these demons and living the life that GOD, the Universe (or whatever higher being) wants for you.

My hope is that my struggles, setbacks, and achievements will inspire you, provide insight on how you can enhance your life, and suggest a multitude of options for your career change. So join me as we experience *Confessions of an Unemployed Professional.*

CHAPTER 1

HOW MISERABLE ARE YOU?

A good job is more than just a paycheck. A good job fosters independence and discipline, and contributes to the health of the community. A good job is a means to provide for the health and welfare of your family, to own a home, and save for retirement.

– JAMES H. DOUGLAS, JR.

EVERYONE'S BEEN THERE: that moment on a Sunday afternoon when you hesitate as you realize the weekend is coming to a close and that dreaded Monday morning is closing in. Pretty soon, you will be at work once again slaving for "the man"—that mythical creature perched in an ivory tower, gazing down upon millions of people addicted to the promise of recognition, job-security, and, if you're lucky, a promotion.

It could be an early morning meeting you dread or a certain co-worker who annoys the crap out of you—doesn't matter; the mere thought of "work" changes your whole mood and those recurring fantasies of walking away from it all comes rushing back. But before you throw in the towel, it's critical for you to ask yourself: "What is this feeling growing at the pit of my stomach really all about? Am I really miserable or am I just annoyed?"

If you are truly unhappy, you must ask yourself how long you plan to continue living a lifestyle that leaves you sad or unsatisfied—or both. If your job is just a temporary means to a weekly or bi-weekly paycheck, then just suck up the discomfort, it will be over soon. But if your job is a stepping-stone along a heavily crafted career plan you devised years ago, then you need to be really honest with yourself and decide whether this career is still right for the rest of your life. If that thought gives you pause or makes you sick, then it's time to find out what is not working.

Is it the people, the work, the commute, that little green troll who shows up every time your boss stretches a 30-minute meeting into a 90-minute borefest? Try to grasp the issues you are struggling with by thoroughly examining what irks you because the truth is this: The problem could actually be *you* and your issues will not disappear if you get another job in another industry, in another city, or in another country. The same issues that bother you now will continue to show up, so don't waste time running from them; stand and face them head-on so they won't hold you back from being the best you can be. Below are some of the areas where you may be having trouble and several suggestions for how to deal with each case.

The Commute

A long, maddening slog into work and then back home can cast a pall on even the most interesting of jobs. How long is your commute? Is it 30 minutes? Major cities with the longest commuting time typically are Los Angeles, San Francisco, New York, and Chicago. Is there a way for you to dodge some of that hassle by working from home during the week, even if just for a day? Ask your boss for this opportunity and, if he consents, then work your butt off the whole day and be sure you are reachable by phone, email, and any instant messaging service your company or organization uses. If your commute really is a major issue with this job, then make sure you are clear about this when evaluating your next job.

The Work

What do you like about the work you do? Is it rewarding and satisfying, or are you bored and wish you had more to do, something with more meat and meaning? The old saying, if you want more work to do, then you first have to do the work they give you perfectly, is very true. Find ways to make your work more interesting. Maybe get to work earlier and really take time to focus and concentrate on the tasks without any distractions from your co-workers. Volunteer for the work no one else wants to do, such as scheduling the company's off-site event, planning the holiday party, or even just ordering lunch on a Friday for the department.

Your Boss

Do you like your boss? More importantly, do you respect your boss? You actually don't have to like your boss, but if you respect him, you can still be a good employee. Do you feel you can depend upon his competence? Did he promise you something yet didn't deliver? Did he give you a bad performance review you think is unwarranted?

I would suggest you set up a 30-minute one-on-one meeting, complete with a detailed agenda, with your boss every week to discuss any issues or concerns you feel need to be addressed. This meeting should be separate from the usual work meetings and is a more personal way to communicate directly. This will show management how you will take the initiative to handle open issues professionally and you care about your job. It also will provide valuable insight into whether your relationship can be improved or is doomed.

It is important for you to determine if this is someone you can work with and trust for some unknown length of time. If you don't feel the relationship can go anywhere but down, then you have to find ways to either work for someone else in the company or start working toward heading out the door for a new opportunity.

Your Colleagues

We don't work with robots; we work with human beings. No matter where you work, you have to deal with unique personalities from a range of different cultures. Working with people is the most challenging aspect of any job, no matter what you do or where you work; however, there are increasingly more jobs that are a great fit for introverts. Please see Appendix D at the end of the book for the top 20 careers perfect for introverts.

Your Attitude

Next, take a good long look at your attitude. Are you grumpy when you arrive at work? Do you even smile at your co-workers? Are you pleasant to your boss or do you project an attitude of someone just picking up a paycheck? Believe it or not, projecting a positive attitude is just as important as a technical skill. People do not like working with others who are irritable and negative or those who never take responsibility for their actions. Take a look at your attitude and make sure you're not negatively influencing others and souring how they relate to you.

Your Competence

Do you feel you can handle your job? Do you feel one step ahead or five steps behind when performing tasks and activities? Be honest with yourself; take the time to objectively look at your work product and identify areas in need of improvement. Could you use additional training to increase your productivity in a certain area, perhaps by taking a class at a local college, or maybe just by watching some online videos?

Regardless of your situation, do not be too quick to jump ship or give up on a stressful situation. Truly evaluate the areas discussed and ask yourself: What is my responsibility and am I doing everything I can do to make this situation better?

After you have honestly re-evaluated your perspective on the problem, check out the 8 red flags that signify it's time for you to go:

- You don't fit in with the corporate culture.
- You don't believe in the company anymore.
- You lack passion for the job.
- Management has stopped giving you new work after you have successfully completed the old assignments.
- Your work environment causes an unnecessary amount of stress and anxiety, which is having negative effects on your health.
- You have no desire to be promoted.
- The company is not doing well and you are constantly in fear of being laid off.
- You have exhausted all avenues to improve the relationship with a co-worker or boss.

For my situation, I felt the biggest challenge rested in the work and the people I worked for. It was no longer rewarding or even manageable for me. The workload became uncontrollable after I was given another unnecessarily complicated project to manage in addition to the other 20 projects I had in flight. To make matters even worse, I was scolded for not being enough of a subject matter expert and for not driving the project forward fast enough.

I met with my direct boss weekly and even my boss's boss to brainstorm ideas on how I could be more successful during my project meetings and how I could mitigate risks and issues more effectively. As I commiserated with the other project managers, I found their frustrations were the same. The project manager is always under the gun and will always be responsible for completing a plethora of activities that are both in and out of his or her control; this is simply the nature of the profession—one I was increasingly questioning as my life's calling.

So after repeated meetings with management to improve my circumstance, and after the 20th work email I sent at midnight, I decided it was best if I left Lexington International and went back to school to explore other options. I was desperately hoping to discover my passion. The only question I had was how the hell I was going to do that.

KEY POINTS TO REMEMBER

- **Evaluate** your work life. Identify what issues are in desperate need of your attention (the commute, the people, your attitude, etc.).

- **Take responsibility and accountability** for the conflicts that you experience. It is up to you to resolve them professionally.

- **Take action** on the conflict or issue, ask to be mentored.

- **Don't stay longer** than two years at a bad job. Knowing when it is time for you to leave is extremely important, because working at a bad job will hurt both your mental and physical health.

CHAPTER 2

FINANCIAL OBLIGATIONS

I finally know what distinguishes man from the other beasts: Financial worries.

– JULES RENARD

IF YOU ARE truly miserable and are trying to leave your current situation, the next question you must answer is this: What do your finances look like at the moment?

First, identify all of your monthly expenses. Financial experts suggest having enough savings to cover your expenses for at least six months; be aware of every penny you spend each month. Also, take a good look at all the elements that make up your net worth.

Your net worth includes any of the following:

- Savings and checking accounts
- 401Ks or IRAs
- Stocks
- Bonds
- Equity on your home and car
- Credit cards
- Any money owed to you

Before I left Lexington International, I reviewed my finances to see how long I could live off of my savings and other assets. I discovered I would be out of money in about four months, including the lump-sum payout for my vacation days. I knew I needed to make a plan and make it quick.

Financial Situation

Are you significantly in debt? Do you have any cash in savings? Do you have a spouse whom may be able to be the primary breadwinner? If so, great, because that means you will still have income coming into your household while you make your job transition. If you are single and you don't have any money saved, then you probably should stick around at your job for at least a few more months while you save some emergency cash and try to pay off any debts you can. Utilize this time to minimize your expenses and plan your exit strategy.

Below is a sample list of monthly expenses. Add up each cost pertaining to you and add any not on this list. Are there any expenses below you can immediately destroy or at least reduce?

- Mortgage or rent payments
- Car loan
- Back taxes
- Child support payments
- Credit card payments
- Traffic tickets
- Car insurance
- Cable and other utility bills
- Food expenses
- Child care

- Cell phone
- School loans

After completing your assessment, if you find you have enough money to support you or your family for 12 months with ease—meaning you don't have to cut back on expenses—then a decision to quit or leave could be realistic. However, this won't be the case for many. If your analysis shows you would struggle financially after two months, then you should review the following options.

Start Working a Side Job

You could begin working another side job before or after work to earn extra money to save for your eventual departure. You have already done your analysis, so you know how much money you need to save before your departure. These jobs could be on-demand jobs that only require a current cell phone, a clean driving record, and a reliable car. What makes these jobs so attractive is the fact you can easily qualify for them and get hired right away. Examples of such jobs are Uber.com, Lyft.com, Postmates.com, and Jolt.com. For more information, please see Chapter 15: The On Demand Economy.

Stay Until You Find a New Job

This is pretty self-explanatory and most of us are taught this when we first enter the workforce—don't leave a job until you have another one lined up. What that means is that you have to just endure the workplace dysfunction and display a positive attitude while posting your resume, networking with various contacts, and going on interviews during your lunch break or vacation days.

Get an Internal Job Transfer

After weeks and weeks, or even months, of trying to improve your current situation, the issues may still not resolved. Subtly, you may want to search other jobs within your current organization or you could be direct with your current boss and see if he/she is open to helping you transfer to a different department. The larger the corporation or business (employees over ten thousand are considered large), the more opportunities there are in the organization. Check your company's internal list of available positions and reach out to internal recruiters hiring for those positions. Also, before you make a decision, discuss with HR the policies for an internal job transfer. Just because you may not have been a match for one department does not mean you will not be better suited for a position somewhere else within the company.

Look for Outside Help

As you work, you pay into the unemployment insurance fund, along with a host of other deductions for things like health insurance and taxes. The amount of unemployment insurance benefits you may qualify for depends on how much money you made in a certain period of time. The maximum amount you can receive in the state of California is $450 a week, and that is before taxes are taken out. Please keep in mind the process for applying for unemployment insurance is different from state to state. Also, you need to have a sufficient reason for leaving a job if you want to be eligible for unemployment benefits. Typically, you will get the benefits if you are completely honest on your application. Be sure to research and understand the rules and regulations. Follow some of the links attached for more information on unemployment insurance benefits.

► https://www.benefits.gov
► http://www.bls.gov/bls/unemployment.htm

See If You Qualify for Short-Term Disability

This option I do not recommend, but if you fit the criteria, here is some information. To claim short-term disability, you need a signed diagnosis from a doctor that you are not in a position to work and therefore will need to claim to be disabled. This can be due to a major stress-related work incident, an accident, or a disaster. In my situation, I qualified because I was on anti-depressants and anti-anxiety medication as a result of stress and exhaustion from working at Lexington International. Typically, you receive short-term disability from the state government. There also is supplemental disability insurance that you can purchase separately from a private company such as Aflac. For more information about disability insurance, please see the links below.

▶ http://www.disabilitysecrets.com/resources/disability/filing-for-disability/eligibility-short-term-disability.htm

▶ http://www.disability-benefits-help.org/   https://www.aflac.com/individuals/products/short-term-disability-insurance.aspx

▶ For California: http://www.edd.ca.gov/Disability/Disability_Insurance.htm

I cannot stress more that being on disability is a lifeline, so don't use it unless you obviously have a long-term disability. Some people will use disability insurance and some people will never use disability. It really is a great service to have for unexpected medical/mental concerns.

Apply for FMLA

This federal law allows you to take a hiatus from your job due to some type of medical situation for a maximum of up to three months to take care of a family member or yourself. You will have to have supporting medical documentation from a doctor to obtain the leave. The act protects your job for up to three months. For more information about FMLA, check out the links below.

- ▶ https://www.dol.gov/whd/fmla

- ▶ https://www.dol.gov/whd/fmlahttps://www.thebalance.com/the-family-and-medical-leave-act-1918631?utm

A Word of Caution

For specific information on your company's benefits, such as unemployment, a leave of absence, etc., talk with a human resources representative whom you trust. If you share this interest with a representative whom may contact your boss about your intentions, this could put you in a very awkward position. Remember, you always want to be in control of your employment, not the other way around.

Plan for an Emergency Plan C

No matter what option you choose, keep in mind your outlook on life will be different when your money is low. The world will all of a sudden become a cold, cruel place when you begin to realize you aren't living like you are accustomed to. What will you do in an emergency? Who will you call?

- Do you have a friend you feel comfortable enough with to borrow money from? Do you have a family member you're on good terms with who can lend you money in a crunch? Have all of these questions answered so you can have some level of confidence and control should the unfortunate happen.

Key Points to Remember

- **Identify** your monthly expenses; know exactly how much is going out each month.

- Research all your options before you leave your job completely; whether you apply for an internal job transfer or apply for FMLA, know exactly what your options are.

- **Identify** all of your assets.

- **Establish** a time frame for how long you think you will be unemployed and then double that figure. Will you be able to handle the stress of surviving a long period of uncertainty?

- **Talk to** your company's human resource representative to understand the particulars about disability and unemployment insurance. There may be some nuanced differences not voluntarily disclosed to employees.

- **Establish** a Plan B and a Plan C—should the worst happen, who can be a lifeline in your support circle?

CHAPTER 3

TIMING IS EVERYTHING

When the seasons shift, even the subtle beginning, the scent of a promised change, I feel something stir inside me. Hopefulness? Gratitude? Openness? Whatever it is, it's welcome.

– KRISTIN ARMSTRONG

AS YOU APPROACH your job search, you should be as strategic as humanly possible. As a project management professional who experienced the negative aspects of unemployment, I am familiar with slow responses from potential employers and slow traction during the employment transition. I discovered there are good times to begin a job search and there are not-so-good times as well.

Obviously, working in a job while testing the waters is the most advantageous situation to be in. Nevertheless, if you don't have a job and need one quickly, then knowing the following can improve your job search and help you maintain your sanity. The following lists describe the characteristics of key hiring time frames throughout the year. All industries have different hiring cycles, but certain times of the year are better for practically every industry.

JANUARY THROUGH MARCH: Happy New Year! Typically, the beginning of the year is a time when corporate budgets have been approved, so significant hiring occurs. This is the point when vacant positions are filled because there is new money in the budget and many frozen positions can now be filled.

Change really will be everywhere, from New Year's resolutions to maternity leaves, this period of time is one of the best windows to find a fantastic new opportunity. If you have a job and are looking for something better, this is a great time to let recruiters and those in your network know you are actively looking for new opportunities.

> **PRO:** One of the best times of the year to look for work because new budgets have been approved to hire for new positions. Besides, who wouldn't want a new better-paying job to help offset all those holiday splurges?

> **CON:** Competition is fierce because hiring managers have been collecting resumes and applications for months. You are not the only who has been looking for a new job.

APRIL THROUGH MAY: Spring is in the air and with every new breeze, new opportunities bloom. This period of time is not quite as intense as the one mentioned above because many open positions from the end of the previous budget year may have been filled, but it is still a great time to continue building your network and researching your potential employer. Don't waste time because summer is coming and summer vacations are right around the corner.

> **PRO:** Still a significant number of jobs to be filled; this is still a great time to move. Put all the networking you did in November/December to work.

> **CON:** Tight time window before summer arrives and responses begin to slow down.

JUNE THROUGH AUGUST: This period can be a frustrating time to be on the job hunt when you are unemployed. According to Boston.com, the summer months bring on the "summer slump" with work productivity decreasing by 20 percent. A hiring manager's priority lists may start with his upcoming vacation, not necessarily with interviewing or filling a few open positions. This is a slow period, so use this time to do your research and build your network.

PRO: There are fewer job seekers to compete with because they may be on vacation. Managers with vacancies may be eager to fill positions because they fear carrying an open job into their company's fourth quarter, when openings often are frozen, is beneficial to reach budget targets.

CON: For some companies, the key hiring professionals may be on vacation, which may delay the interview process.

SEPTEMBER THROUGH OCTOBER: Welcome to fall! With the leaves turning colors and the winds of change swirling to and fro, this is a good time to test the waters. This is the beginning of a new school year so at least new teachers are receiving employment. The end of the year is right around the corner and companies will pull out all the stops to add more resources to get undelivered work completed before the year ends. Also, during this time some companies will start closing their annual books. This means hiring is in demand to add additional contractors, managers, and general staff to complete as much work as possible before the year ends. Some companies may also enter into a hiring freeze for the fourth quarter, so the desire to hire during this period is crucial to get any leftover work completed.

PRO: Great time to start a job search; the year is winding down and companies are under pressure to reach critical business goals before the year ends. A last-minute hiring wave to complete open business objectives is guaranteed.

CON: There is only a limited window of time to find a job quickly before the holidays arrive. Winter is coming.

NOVEMBER THROUGH DECEMBER: During this time of year, there is great change. People leave jobs desperately seeking new opportunities, some employees are let go, and some people abandon ship for an ocean liner. However, if you have a job but want something better, then starting a job search in December can be advantageous. "December could even be the best time of year to start looking for a job," Joanie Ruge, senior vice president at Adecco Group North America, a unit of the world's largest employment staffing firm, told CNN Money.com. With an abundance of parties and events in the works, "it's a great time to be networking because most companies want to get people on board in January," she stated. Just be aware this is a time for networking; don't expect to start a new job immediately in December.

If you want a decent job fast, then starting your job search during this time period will only frustrate you. At this time of year, many corporate organizations may be consumed with closing out the books and planning the budget for the next year. However, if you just want some extra cash, doing seasonal work is a great opportunity. Chances are you will be working in retail or utilizing the on-demand economy.

PRO: Good potential to network with people due to all the holiday parties. You may snag yourself some interviews in the New Year.

CON: This is a bad time to find a full-time job quickly. There are too many holiday parties and scheduled vacations tend to slow the job recruitment process down to a grinding halt.

KEY POINTS TO REMEMBER

- **Identify** the best time of year to increase your chances of getting hired quickly.

- **Evaluate** the windows of time when jobs are plentiful and employers are very eager for new employees.

- The holiday season is a good time to **network** due to holiday parties and impromptu social gatherings.

- Use slow periods to **meet** people, increase your network, and to target the specific type of job you really want.

CHAPTER 4

FROM PAIN TO PASSION

Passion is one great force that unleashes creativity, because if you're passionate about something, then you're more willing to take risks.

– YO-YO MA

I REMEMBER SITTING in that monthly workstream meeting on a cloudy day in August. My thoughts were racing. "Why am I here? Am I being punked or punished? What is my crime and how long is my sentence? Is this work part of my life's goals? What is my purpose?"

I could not help but believe my life's purpose coincided with whatever desires I had in life—the desire to create, to write a book, to own a franchise, to create an app, to write a song, to work in the tech industry. All I knew was I wanted to do something creative, something in which I could use more of my own innate ingenuity. As I approached my 33rd birthday, I deemed all the joy from my soul would be sucked away if I remained in my current situation.

I made the decision to leave Lexington International and signed up for Entertainment Studies at the UCLA Extension Program (https://www.uclaextension.edu/). The first class I took was an improvisation class, which kept me in a constant state of fear. The class forced me outside my comfort zone in front of strangers, freeing me and allowing me to become more comfortable around uncertainty.

Was it my passion? I don't know, but I was happier than I had been in years, especially when I was permitted to be creative and express myself. The program consisted of acting, writing, digital marketing, and everything I loved. I only prayed it was leading me to my passion.

What is your passion? Below are some ideas for how to identify your unique areas of interests that could lead to cultivating more passion in your life for both work and play.

Identify Your Natural Talents

What are the subjects that got you As from elementary school through high school? What tests did you take that you aced and didn't study for? If you can't come up with anything specific, then ask a family member or some friends who know you well. Do you remember the list of rewards you obtained as a child? Did you win 1st, 2nd, or 3rd place at the science fair? Did you win a trophy on the debate team, and no I'm not talking about that ribbon they give out for just showing up.

Take a walk down memory lane and review your earliest achievements.

List 5 activities you enjoyed as a child.

1. _____

2. _____

3. _____

4. _____

5. _____

What did you get in trouble for?

Did you like sports? Did you leave your baseball and football gear all around the house? Did you like to paint or draw, but got paint everywhere and your mother always fussed, so you stopped painting? Did you like to tinker in the basement for long hours with wires, tape, and batteries, yet got yelled at for not washing the dishes? Did you crack jokes in class and was scolded by the teacher? These could be areas you should research more thoroughly to see where it leads you; you may discover a hidden talent that can be marketed.

List 5 actions you repeatedly got in trouble for as a child.

1. _____

2. _____

3. _____

4. _____

5. _____

What Makes You Lose Track of Time?

What can you do that makes the hours zoom by at the speed of light? Do you like to paint, dance, sing, read, or write? Typically, this means you are so present in the moment that space and time are irrelevant. Do more of this and you will be surprised at how your life will respond.

List 3 activities that allow you to lose track of time.

1. _____

2. _____

3. _____

Check Out Assessment, Personality, and Passion Tests

Check out the passion test developed by Chris and Janet Bray Attwood. The passion test is meant "to help you discover your passions and begin really living" and is available in multiple formats, including a book, eBook, online course, and a teleseminar. Online content is available at http://PassionTest.com/.

If you want to gain insight on your personality and see what other jobs might be a good fit for your personality type, then look into the Myers Briggs test. This test can help you identify your temperament and discover if you are an introvert or an extrovert.

- **Introverts:** An introvert is an individual who processes information deeply and thoughtfully. Many times these individuals are considered shy or reserved because they can get caught up with thoughts in their head. Truth is, introverts simply process energy differently. Social interactions typically drain introverts leading them to need solitude to recharge.

- **Extroverts:** Extroverts are basically the opposite of introverts. They crave, even thrive, social interaction, as it energizes their passion and creativity. Solitude for them would be draining and depressive. The following link, http://www.

myersbriggs.org/my-mbti-personality-type/mbti-basics/extraversion-or-introversion.htm, will provide more information on introversion and extroversion spectrums.

Also, if you would like to map your aptitude for different professions, check out http://assessment.com/. This website has over 70 questions to complete before you receive a free MAPP sample report, which matches you to five different careers.

Get More Training or a Certification

A certification can also be an affordable way to gain quick credibility in a new profession. Certificate programs are "a solution for those who want to get a short-term, highly career-oriented, compressed program to get out into the job market," says Carol Aslanian, senior vice president of market research at EducationDynamics, a higher education marketing company. Utilize the following link for information on certifications: http://www.usnews.com/education/online-education/articles/2010/03/26/online-certificate-programs-offer-a-fast-track-to-a-new-career

If you are receiving unemployment insurance in California, you may qualify for additional training of up to $6,000. If you want training, you must contact the EDD (Employment Development Department) within 16 months of becoming unemployed.

- Take the time to explore what you truly want to do. Regardless of what it is, the key is to take action and do something. For me, after I finished several classes at the UCLA extension program, I began working a series of contract jobs with several local Fortune 500 companies in Los Angeles, California. This proved to be a great financial gain because the compensation I received was very competitive; however, I was still on the lookout for a long-term permanent position.

KEY POINTS TO REMEMBER

- **Identify** your natural talents by remembering your childhood achievements and failures. Ask others what they think you excel at; you may be surprised by the responses.

- **Obtain** a certification in a new profession to gain credibility.

- **Identify** activities where time seemed to slip away. Take the time to increase those activities.

- **Take** some personality, aptitude, or passion tests.

CHAPTER **5**

WHAT TYPE OF JOB DO YOU WANT NEXT?

*If you want to succeed, you should strike out on new paths,
rather than travel the worn paths of accepted success.*

– JOHN D. ROCKEFELLER

NOW THAT YOU have a better idea of what you are interested in doing, see where that interest may fit within the following industries:

- Healthcare
- Technology
- Solar/Energy
- Customer Relations
- Manufacturing
- Automotive
- Finance
- Engineering

You can research additional industries at http://www.careerinfonet.org/indview1.asp?nodeid=45 if these are not interesting to you. Also, for additional information concerning pertinent industry and/or job title information for salary, skills, or even diverse job titles, research www.labormarketinfo.edd.ca.gov or www.onetonline.org/. After you have a better idea of the industry to pursue, determine the job category you are seeking: a part-time job, a temporary job, a contract job, or a full-time job.

Part-time Jobs

This type of job offers work with fewer than the standard 40 hours per week. The number of hours worked each week can range from 2 to 30 hours. Depending on the position, the pay can range anywhere from $8 to $19 per hour, and some positions do come with health benefits. A lot of part-time work is available in the retail and hospitality industries, though other industries may participate in partial employment.

The companies listed below are always looking for part-time employees

- Wal-Mart
- Starbucks
- McDonalds
- Target
- Bed Bath and Beyond
- Walgreens
- Rite Aid
- Panera Bread
- Best Western Hotels
- Howard Johnson

PRO: Part-time jobs can be a great way to make money when you are in school and/or in between a full-time job. They can also serve as great exposure for a new career or profession.

CON: The pay is low and typically these jobs have a high turn-over rate.

Temporary Jobs

These jobs can last anywhere from 2 weeks to 3 months with pay anywhere from $10-$25 an hour, depending on the position. A lot of companies use temp employees for positions like administrative assistants, executive assistants, receptionists, filing, and other administrative opportunities. The companies listed below are temp agencies that supply temporary employees to companies with a need, but always check out the nearest location in your area.

- ManPower.com
- RobertHalfInternational.com
- Addecco.com
- Randstad.com
- Spherionstaffing.com
- Kellyservices.com
- Aerotek.com

PRO: Temporary jobs can be a nice way to make enough money to pay the bills, while also exploring different types of jobs without having to commit to a particular company or organization. The temporary job can also expose you to new skills or working with a new piece of technology/equipment.

CON: A lot of corporations and organizations have had less than positive experiences with temporary employees. Since the job is temporary, some temps do not behave in a professional manner (showing up late, not coming into work, leaving work without informing anyone, etc.). Please don't exhibit these traits. Whatever job you get is a reflection of you and your brand. Do your best and be professional so you don't make it harder for other job seekers to get a good job.

Contract/Consulting Job

A contract/consulting job is one you get from a consulting agency. The difference between a contract job and a temporary job is a contract job requires very specific requirements, meaning more experience in a specialized field such as technology, engineering, finance, or healthcare. These jobs are highly competitive and provide significant compensation.

PRO: The benefit of a contract job is the pay range is much greater than for temporary positions. The pay range can be anywhere from $30 to $150, depending on the position you are applying for and your skill level.

CON: You are not a full-time employee, thus you will not receive healthcare benefits, a yearly bonus, or vacation days. Also, depending on the company or organization, a contractor can be treated like a second-class citizen who gets paid well.

Listed below are several of the most popular and largest contract agencies in the U.S. Check out the nearest location in your area.

- Accenture
- Bain & Company
- Deloitte Consulting
- PricewaterhouseCoopers
- Ernest & Young
- Cornerstone Research

- McKinsey & Co.
- Booz Allen
- Brattle Group

Full-time or Permanent Job

As a full-time employee, you receive healthcare benefits, an annual bonus, vacation/sick days, and a retirement program. Additionally, you may be invited to the company picnic, all-hands meetings, and the annual Christmas party if your company participates in these or other bonuses.

PRO: You are a part of a community and an organization and, as the years go by, you really can see an accumulation of wealth and health benefits.

CON: You have to complete yearly/annual reviews and listen to counsel on how you can improve. You may have to deal with an emotional and financial outcome if your company has unexpected/massive layoffs.

KEY POINTS TO REMEMBER

- **Research** your industry and apply it to your interests and possible passion.

- **Determine** what type of job you want (part-time, contract, temporary, or full-time).

- **Reach out** directly to companies that have part-time work.

- **Reach out** directly to temporary and consulting agencies.

CHAPTER 6

DAILY ROUTINE

One of the things I learned the hard way was that it doesn't pay to get discouraged. Keeping busy and making optimism a way of life can restore your faith in yourself.

LUCILLE BALL

NOW THAT YOU are no longer a slave to the daily grind, you have immense freedom to do as you choose. However, this freedom comes with a cost; if you abuse the freedom, it will lead to wasted time and possibly depression.

To prevent this, I would suggest creating your own daily schedule. Set a time to get up out the bed every day. Maybe it's at 8:30 or 9:30 a.m.; just pick a time and stick to it every day. This will guard against that one day where you don't get out of bed and sleep until noon as well as helping to minimize the guilt from being free while others are working.

Keep Busy

Another thing is to create a To-Do list. I would suggest writing out the list the night before. The To-Do list should have at least 25 items to check off. Now, you may not get to complete all 25 things, but it doesn't matter. Just check off what you did complete and move the open items to the next day. This act will build organization in your life and boost your self-esteem; it also reinforces a sense of productivity.

As a part of your daily schedule, you will want to make room for some social interaction. You will no longer have those co-workers who you could bitch to about the boss or the idiot director or even ask about the latest episode of *Scandal*. Not only will you be alone, but if you also thought the world revolved around you, then you're in for a rude awakening. The world will continue to keep spinning on without you, now that you're free of the rat race.

Furthermore, don't be surprised if the co-worker you thought was such a great friend no longer returns your calls now that you're gone. As you have left the company, your former coworker/friend feels he/she no longer needs to be in your life. So get out of the house and make new friends by any means necessary.

Whatever You Do, Get Out of the House

- **Take a class:** In Chapter 4, we talked about the possibility of taking a class to acquire new or additional training. This will provide a great opportunity to meet new people and discover new places.

- **Meet with friends/family once a week:** Make the visit a weekly occurrence so it's something you look forward to several times a month.

- **Party:** Go out to parties and introduce yourself to people. When the subject of your occupation comes up, explain by saying you just completed an assignment and you're evaluating your next challenge. Talk about what you're looking for, but do not ask for a job.

- **Go to the movies:** I hope you're not one of those people who can only go to the movies with other people. If you are, you're missing out. I've been going to a movie by myself for a while, especially when a good film I've been looking forward to seeing is playing. Go see a matinee show for $5 or $6, remembering you are on a budget. It will help break up the monotony of your week and allow you to relax and enjoy for about two hours.

- **Join a gym:** Staying physical is going to be very important now—you need to keep moving. Join a gym within your budget; it's worth it. Not only will it be a great source of physical activity, but it will also be a place you can go and interact with people daily without spending extra money. Investigate http://Groupon.com or http://livingSocial.com/ as they may have a deal with no sign-up fee.

- **Go to the bookstore/library:** Utilize those tax dollars at your local library that has an impressive selection of resources whether DVDs, books, access to Wi-Fi, books-on-tape, and any other classes or programs you can attend. If you do not have a library card, all you need to do is show two proofs of local residence and a valid ID. Many major bookstores also provide seminars or lectures that may assist you to find your next endeavor as well as providing the most up-to-date reading materials to utilize. Another useful resource is Amazon.com in which you may purchase new or used books for career or occupational research.

- **Do volunteer or charity work:** This activity will help you get out of your own head and remind you there are plenty of other people who have it a lot worse than you. It also provides a great opportunity to network with new people not to mention just great Karma to put out into the Universe. Check out Craigslist.org in your area for areas to volunteer.

KEY POINTS TO REMEMBER

- **Maintain** a standing weekly visit with friends and family.

- **Keep busy** tackling errands and chores you put off for the last six months.

- **Join** a gym to keep active.

- **Go** to the library or the local bookstore and take advantages of all your resources available to you.

- **Purchase** new and used books on Amazon.

- Do volunteer or charity work – **be altruistic.**

CHAPTER **7**

THE UNEMPLOYED WORK WEEK

A day of worry is more exhausting than a week of work.

– JOHN LUBBOCK

A S YOU CONDUCT your job search, you will begin to notice a pattern from week to week, specifically from Sunday to Saturday. To make the weeks as productive as possible, I recommend trying to front-load the beginning of each week, meaning plant as many seeds as possible at the start of the week to get the maximum amount of momentum going. That way, by Thursday and Friday you can accept invites for interviews and close out the week with a sense of productivity and accomplishment.

Listed below is a pattern for each day of the week.

Sunday

This is a great day to write out your To-Do list for the week. Use this day to research information on the companies you are interested in working for. Plan for networking and use sites like https://www.meetup.com and https://www.eventbrite.com to discover key networking opportunities. Additionally, upload your resume to as many job boards (Linkedin.com, Indeed.com, Monster.com, Careerbuilder.com, etc.) as you can. When recruiters run their weekly reports from various job boards, your resume will show up first in the listings on Monday morning.

Monday

Mondays can be slow, as employees are either coming into work late or have a slew of back-to-back meetings before they can get any real work done. Luckily, you have already emailed recruiters and uploaded your resume to the job boards on Sunday, so your name is high on their return call list.

Tuesday

Tuesdays are great for following up with networking and business contacts. Usually, calls will be conducted between the hours of 9:30 and 11:30 in the morning and then once again after 1:30 pm. There is movement on Tuesdays because usually the hiring manager has had time to review several resumes and reach out to a recruiter or directly to a potential candidate.

Wednesday

Hump Day—Try to get in as much work as possible on Wednesday. This is really the heart of the week. There is pressure to have decisions made about which candidates will move forward with an interview and which will be rejected. Be extremely proactive on this day and connect with past colleagues on LinkedIn.

Thursday

Thursday is your last shot to seal the deal. Follow up with all of your contacts through email, phone calls, information posted on LinkedIn, and do it early. The week is coming to an end and hiring managers are starting to plan their weekend. Unless the position is critical, the goal of hiring potential candidates will be placed on the back burner.

Friday

Hopefully, the hiring manager went to work. On Fridays, the hiring team is not thinking about scheduling interviews. I may be exaggerating a bit, but Fridays can be very slow and dead in certain organizations. So please don't expect major productivity today. Typically, the phone will not ring as expected and, if it does, it will be about something happening next week.

Saturday

As much as we love weekends, when you are unemployed, they are not welcomed. They simply slow down the job-search momentum. Use this day to rest, relax, and rejuvenate. This can be the day to have coffee or drinks with a friend, go to a movie, or do anything that will reinvigorate your spirit for the week ahead.

KEY POINTS TO REMEMBER

- Use Sunday to **prepare** for the week ahead by sending emails, uploading resumes to job boards, and writing out your To-Do list.

- Keep in mind that Monday and Tuesdays can be slow, but are a great time to send emails, leave voice mails, and research potential employers.

- **Build up** the momentum for each week by front-loading all of your job-search activities at the start, so everything will come together by Thursday and Friday.

- Use Saturday to **rest and relax**. This can be the time to have coffee or drinks with a friend.

CHAPTER **8**

IS IT TIME TO RELOCATE?

Circumstances in life often take us places that we never intended to go. We visit some places of beauty, others of pain and desolation.

– KRISTIN ARMSTRONG

A S YOU THINK about specific industries and businesses to work for, you might find they are not in your current location. Within the United States, there are certain industries more prevalent in certain regions of the country. Listed below are examples of the top industries in four regions in America—the South, the North, the Midwest, and the West Coast.

I wanted to stay on the West Coast because, although California is expensive, I wanted to be near the action—the action for technology that is. The hottest place to be for technology is the area from Silicon Valley to San Francisco. Feel free to checkout the cost of living in various areas within the U.S. Below is a list of links that provide current information on cost of living data in the U.S.

- ▶ http://www.bankrate.com
- ▶ http://www.Salary.com/
- ▶ http://www.Payscale.com/
- ▶ http://www.glassdoor.com/

The Southeast

Generally, the southeastern states stretch from Louisiana to Georgia, as far south as Florida to as far north as Virginia. Manufacturing is immense in the Southeast, with states like Georgia, Alabama, and Mississippi having huge automobile plants like Mercedes Benz, Hyundai, and Toyota. The Southeast is also home to some of the top banking corporations including Bank of America, Regions Financial Corporate, Am South Bancorporation, BBVA Compass in Birmingham, and Sun Trust Bank. Georgia also has a booming entertainment industry that includes studios for music, TV, and film. Such popular studios as Tyler Perry Studios, Pinewood Studio, and EUE/Screen Gems in Atlanta are major competitors to the Los Angeles studios.

The North

The northern states stretch from Maryland to Maine and from Washington D.C. to as far west as Chicago. Banking and trading are huge in the northern states, especially with Wall Street in New York, which many people consider the most powerful city in America, if not the world. Additionally, the capital of America, Washington D.C., is also known as the Hollywood for ugly people. You also have a lot of extremely prestigious colleges and universities in Boston and Pennsylvania, with schools such as Harvard, Princeton, and Yale.

The Midwest

The Midwest region could be called the Land of Farms. It is one of the most important farming areas in the United States and consists of 12 states including Illinois, Indiana, Iowa, Kansas, Michigan, Minnesota, Missouri, Nebraska, North Dakota, Ohio, South Dakota, and Wisconsin. Twenty-seven Midwestern companies were among the top 100 largest U.S. companies in 2015, according to the Midwest Governor's Association. The top-traded industries in the region are in production technology and heavy machinery, food processing and manufacturing, printing services, transportation and logistics, automotive, and chemical product development.

In this region, the top companies include General Motors in Detroit, Ford Motor Co. in Michigan, Proctor and Gamble in Cincinnati, Ohio, Caterpillar and U.S. Foods in Illinois, Owens Corning in Toledo, Ohio, and Whirlpool in Benton Harbor, Michigan.

The West Coast

The West Coast stretches from Oregon to Southern California including Hollywood and San Diego, which are vast industries in tourism, film, television, music, arts, real estate, cuisine, and law and legal services, given the numerous amounts of people who reside in the area.

Northern California consists of the booming Silicon Valley and historic San Francisco scene. Silicon Valley is a conglomeration of cities including Menlo Park, Palo Alto, San Jose, Mountain View, and Cupertino. Here you will find mega-tech companies like Facebook, Google, Samsung, and Pinterest. If you want to be surrounded by an industry that is full of young grads hell-bent on changing the world with the next disruptive technology, then Silicon Valley is the place for you. Just keep in mind it is expensive to live in Northern California.

Other parts of the West Coast include Seattle, Portland, and Anchorage. There are many industries available in each city in which you may want to research if you are having an issue finding work in your own state. In Seattle, major industries include engineering, architecture, advanced manufacturing, and education, to name a few. Up to the north of the United States, such as in Portland and other cities in Oregon, you will find professions in education, technology, business such as management and administration, as well as transportation and utilities. If you are looking for a career farther north in Alaska, you will find an abundance of positions in communications, finance, and logistics.

KEY POINTS TO REMEMBER

- Do your **research** on where your industry will make you happiest.

- **Research** the cost of living with http://www.bankrate.com/calculators/savings/moving-cost-of-living-calculator.aspx, salary.com or glassdoor.com.

- **Prepare** for a culture shock when moving from one major region to another.

- **Don't limit yourself** to what you've heard about a particular region – sample it for yourself.

- The regions of America are all different with specific nuances.

- If you are the adventurous type, don't be afraid to pack up and move to another state.

- **Don't limit** your next job to your hometown or where you went to high school or college.

CHAPTER **9**

MARKETING MATERIALS

If you call failures experiments, you can put them in your resume and claim them as achievements.

– MASON COOLEY

IREMEMBER WHEN I was in high school and during the summers of college, I would go through the phone book and call hundreds of companies to see if they were hiring for office positions. In today's professional world, it's all about being online and having a professional Internet presence.

Employers want to know if you are technologically astute and current with the latest trends. They want your Facebook page to be interesting, but not too wild and your LinkedIn page to be up-to-date, professional, and crisp. Below are some suggestions for helping you improve your internet presence.

Update Your Resume

Your resume is a snapshot of your professional employments, skills, and accomplishments. Hiring managers use your resume to evaluate if you will be a good candidate for employment in their company, thus you should have a resume that clearly defines who you are and how valuable you will be for employment. There are two different formats for resumes: a functional resume and a chronological resume.

The Functional Resume: A functional resume lists the work you have done in order of function. If, for example, you are a project manager, all of your project management work experience is grouped together. If you've also done some engineering work, then that would be grouped separately. The companies you worked for would be listed separately and not in chronological order. Examples of a functional resume can be found at

▶ http://www.monster.com/career-advice/article/Sample-of-a-Functional-Resume.

The Chronological Resume: This resume lists your work experience in order of occurrence, with dates associated with each job in chronological order. For examples of a Chronological resume see the following links:

▶ http://img.docstoccdn.com/thumb/orig/12403362.png

▶ http://www.hireme101.com/images/chronologicalresume.jpg

▶ http://img.docstoccdn.com/thumb/orig/12403362.png

The rule with resumes is simple: revise, revise, and then revise some more. You really must adopt the mindset to update your resume continuously over the next three months. You want the resume to be as crisp and concise as possible. Hire someone to review your resume and offer critiques. You can find a host of freelance resume writers on sites like Guru.com, Uplink.com, and fiverr.com. Freelancers will bid for your project and you can select the best one based on their expertise and price.

Posting Your Resume

Use job boards to get the attention of recruiters nationwide. Create a profile and upload your resume on sites like the ones listed below. In the profile, be specific about what type of job you're looking for such as contract, full-time, or temporary and in which industry or field. Recruiters both nationwide and worldwide check these sites daily for a new pool of applicants.

- Indeed.com
- Monster.com
- Careerbuilders.com
- Simply Hired.com
- Dice.com
- USAJobs.com
- The EDD Resume Website
- Americasjobcenter.ca.gov (applies to whatever state you're in)

Clean Up Your Facebook Page

Recruiters and potential employers do look at your online presence, so I recommend cleaning up your Facebook page, certainly taking down any overtly obscene pictures or comments. I would really advise having two accounts: one for your family and school friends, and then another page in which you can be more open and uncensored.

Use LinkedIn

You must create a LinkedIn profile because it is your online resume. The benefit is you can add an abundant amount of other information to underscore your value and enhance your appeal.

LinkedIn also allows you to upload PowerPoint slides to highlight previous work assets, upload videos to showcase your personality, or even create blog posts on topics you are passionate about. Please make sure you take a professional picture of yourself; you can do this with your cellphone, but ensure there is good lighting and you look professional.

You also may want to join professional groups that coincide with the field you work in. For example, if you're a project manager, join a project management work group. You can ask questions and post discussion topics to engage other members. You can also purchase the premium membership on LinkedIn for $29.99 a month, which provides advantages such as the ability to directly contact recruiters who are not in your network, get moved to the top of the recruiter's applicant list, see who who's viewed your profile in the last 90 days, and see how you compare to other applicants in your field. You will also receive access to online courses from Lynda.com.

Recruiters/Head Hunters

There are two types of recruiters, internal recruiters and external recruiters. Internal recruiters are specific to a certain company. They hire directly for the company and typically have special relationships with hiring managers company-wide. External recruiters are usually with an agency that contracts or has arrangements with larger organizations to fill staffing needs. The key difference is external recruiters have multiple clients or businesses they work with, therefore they are usually aware of multiple job opportunities from various organizations.

By using recruiters, you not only learn about the job presented to you, but also what skills specific companies are looking for, the range of what they are paying, and the current trends in your profession. Develop a genuine rapport with recruiters if you can because they are a wealth of information. What you are doing now is what they do for a living, so try to pick the brains of the experts.

Most likely recruiters in your field will contact you about how great your resume is and claim they would love to work with you. This is great if they can help you secure a job interview, but don't invest too much time and energy on recruiters. Remember, they are only interested in you if they believe they can make money by selling your skills to a client. Instead, use them to obtain information about current trends in local industries.

Create a Cover Letter and an Elevator Pitch

Don't spend time buying a book on cover letters; instead, Google "cover letter" and decide from the thousands of samples out there which one works for you. Or you can just check out this link for samples:

▶ http://www.monster.com/career-advice/cover-letter-resume/cover-letter-samples

Cover letters do matter, but I found that applying for jobs online is ineffective. The absolute best way to find a job is to network. However, before you do that you need to understand who you are and how you can present that to someone effectively.

The Elevator Pitch

The elevator pitch is a description of your skills, abilities, and accomplishments wrapped up in a 30-second commercial. Below is an example of an elevator pitch for project management.

"Let me give you an example of one of my most successful projects. I was leading a virtual team across three competing companies in a project mandated by the European Regulatory Agency. My role was to plan and lead the monthly meetings where we decided how to test and validate our methods and where the labs compared their data. I am happy to report we came up with a methodology that became an international standard, despite one company's up-front stated goal of dragging the project out as long as possible. My name is _____, and I am interested in taking on scientific challenges in an emerging biotech firm."

For more examples of elevator pitches use the link:

▶ http://improvandy.com/elevator-pitch/examples-of-a-30-sec-ond-elevator-pitch/

KEY POINTS TO REMEMBER

- **Determine** what resume type is best for your industry (Functional or Chronological).

- Pay someone, or at least get several pairs of eyes to review/**edit your resume**.

- **Develop** your elevator pitch by practicing very direct descriptions of experiences highlighting your abilities.

- **Use** recruiters to obtain information about current trends in local professions/industries.

- **Use** LinkedIn to search and apply for jobs and to accumulate recruitment contacts; use them to discover and stay current on industry trends.

CHAPTER **10**

TIME TO LAUNCH

The way to get started is to quit talking and begin doing.

– WALT DISNEY

IN CHAPTER 5, we discussed the different types of jobs available for you to apply for, so by now you should have a clearer idea of what job you desire. In this chapter, we will discuss different strategies for your job hunt. As technology continues to advance, new methods and techniques for job searches are continually evolving.

Job Boards

I recommend uploading a new resume to a job posting website every week on a Sunday night. That way, when recruiters/headhunters run their programs for new potential job matches on Monday morning, your name will show up at the top of the list of potential candidates.

Use Social Media

Create a couple of posts detailing what job you are seeking and some of your skills. Post them on Facebook.com, LinkedIn.com, and Twitter.com. You never know who might be looking for exactly what you have to provide. You can also join groups on Facebook or LinkedIn specific to the position you seek. These groups can help you with advice on your job search and also are perfect for networking.

Use Pain Letters

Employment guru Liz Ryan explains one of her favorite strategies for landing a job in her Forbes article, "What's a Pain Letter and Can It Get Me a Job".

Identify a list of companies you would like to work for, maybe 5 or 10. Then, for each one of those companies, find a hiring manager using LinkedIn. Do research on that hiring manager and investigate what pain points you think they might be experiencing. The key here is to identify ways your experience could help you resolve them. The next step is to craft a letter detailing how your background and expertise could assist with the manager's day-to-day challenges. For more information on Pain Letters, please check out the following link:

▶ http://www.forbes.com/sites/lizryan/2015/06/06/whats-a-pain-letter-and-can-it-get-me-a-job/

Apply to Online Job Applications

This is one of the least popular and, some would say, least effective ways to get a job. Not only are you competing with hundreds of other applicants, but also the computer software selects resumes based on the hot keywords at the moment. Also, companies purposely set up the application to take anywhere from 30 to 45 minutes; this way, they can weed out the applicants whom do not have the determination or stamina to complete the application.

Go to Staffing Agencies/Consulting Agencies Directly

Find staffing agencies by looking at the job boards for whom is posting jobs. Keep in mind that sometimes jobs are not posted immediately. By reaching out to the agency directly, you can get a competitive advantage over other candidates.

Friends and Family

Reach out to friends and family and let them know you are looking for a new employer. The feeling of embarrassment may be there, but everyone has been in your position at some point. However, you need to move on from that feeling and let them know you are actively looking and make sure they know what type of job you are looking for.

Networking

Like most people, I hate networking. For most of my life, I really didn't understand what it was. Networking is really nothing more than building a rapport with a stranger and making a significant enough connection for him or her to remember you.

There is no need to feel pressure to ask for something. Just be yourself and focus on making a connection. The only result you may want to obtain from the interaction is contact information such as a phone number, an email address, a Facebook profile, or a LinkedIn connection.

Networking can be done at any time and anywhere. You can make conversation with someone at the gym, waiting in line at the store or post office, or even at the DMV. The key is to not be afraid to make a comment, ask a question, compliment a stranger, or simply smile. We live in an intense culture that is leery of strangers. If you speak up, people may think you are a threat, a solicitor, or you're some weirdo forcing them out of their comfort zone. Don't be afraid to be that weirdo; talk to strangers and you will be amazed at how much you can learn.

Initiate an Informational Interview

Find people who you respect or admire and offer to take him or her out for coffee or lunch. You may find these people on Facebook, LinkedIn, or a friend of a friend. The key is to have a plan. Know why you want to talk and what you want to talk to him or her about. You may be asking for advice on a career move, career direction, the current environment of the retail business, or something else. The purpose is to obtain information that can better assist your job search. This is not the time to ask for a job. Listed below are some questions you can ask during the informational interview.

1.   What type of educational background or certification is required for this job?

2.   What is the most satisfying aspect of this job?

3.   What entry-level jobs are best to learn about in this field?

4.   Do you recommend speaking with anyone else about this job/industry?

5.   How can I become more marketable in this field?

Use Your High School or College Alumni Network

Use that elevator speech, any fraternity or social clubs, and talk to your friends, your in-laws, the local EDD office, and everybody. You never know where or from whom your next opportunity will come. For even more suggestions and ideas, just simply look up "how to find a job" on YouTube. There are many new and unique ideas that people are trying every day.

KEY POINTS TO REMEMBER

- **Use** social media to let your online friends know what job you're seeking.

- **Upload** a new resume at least once a week to move up high on a recruiter's search results.

- **Use** staffing/temporary agencies to apply for jobs that may not be posted yet.

- **Use** the pain letter approach to position yourself for a job with less competition.

- **Networking** is all about building rapport with strangers.

- **Network** with family, friends, high school/college alumni, and anywhere and everywhere – at the bank, at the gym, or even the grocery store.

- **Completing** applications online is the least-effective method of seeking a new job.

CHAPTER **11**

NAVIGATING THE INTERVIEW PROCESS

I guess the best advice I ever got or anyone could get for doing a talk show, though it has not been easy very often, was from Jack Paar, who said, 'Kid, don't make it an interview. Interviews have clipboards, and you're like David Frost. Make it a conversation.'

– DICK CAVETT

YOU ARE NOT alone if you dread interviewing. A significant number of professionals dread the process of bragging about himself or herself to a complete stranger and then are scrutinized repeatedly. I think it can be helpful to deconstruct the interview process and arm yourself with tips, techniques, and a lot of practice. Review the sections below, which are designed to prepare you for real-world situations.

Interview Types

By now, you have completed applications online and have uploaded your resume to multiple job boards. You will start to get calls from both internal and external recruiters and at this point you need to be ready for an interview. Today, companies are increasingly using telephone interviews as their main method of screening applicants. Some companies even have a pre-screen in front of their phone for maximum efficiency. So be prepared.

The online video conferencing interview is becoming increasingly popular. Therefore, you need to be comfortable with an online video conferencing interview. Make sure all the necessary software is installed in advance of your interview; finding out you need to install additional software five minutes before your interview is not professional and may automatically result in a disqualification.

Initial Interview Preparation

Before the initial interview, research the company by doing an internet search. Additionally, you should have a formal job description that lists all the duties and responsibilities for the position you are applying. The job description can be found where the position was posted or from the recruiter who contacted you. I would suggest creating a job description matrix that lists the responsibilities/requirements on one side and how your experiences match with them on the other side. See the diagram listed in Appendix E. This will be a document you can take with you to provide to the interviewer.

Questions, Questions, Questions

Be prepared to answer and ask questions regarding the role you are seeking. The following lists show 10 general questions you could be asked (with corresponding suggested answers) and 10 questions you can ask your potential employer about your role and the company.

10 Questions You Could Be Asked

1. **Why do you want to work at XY Company?**

    You want to work at the company because you believe it is the perfect place to expand your career.

    You have to research the company enough to know at least two examples of success the company has accomplished in the last 6 months. The interviewer is simply trying to access your interest and how much research you conducted on the company.

2. **What are five of your strengths?**

    The interviewer is accessing your self-awareness. Do you know yourself? You will have to communicate this to the interviewer in a confident way without being too arrogant.

3. **What is one of your weaknesses?**

    Ideally, this is similar to the previous question. However, this question can be your downfall. The trick is to never pick a weakness that would turnoff your interviewer. Instead, choose something that seems to be a weakness, but put a positive spin on it such as I sometimes take longer to finish a project than I should because of my meticulous level of detail.

4. **Why did you leave your last job?**

    This can be a loaded question, as you want to be honest, yet cautious. Your response will be a reflection of you as an employee and how well you can work with management and other employees. You can respond by saying your assignment ended because it was a temporary or contract assignment, you left to pursue other challenges, you chose to return to school to further your education, or even more specifically the department was going through a series of changes, making it very difficult for one to be successful in the organization.

5. **Tell me a situation in which you went above and beyond what was expected.**

    This question allows you to look back at your past and think of a time you simply gave more than expected. Maybe you stepped in at the last minute to help schedule the Christmas party or you volunteered to run the blood drive or even noticed a gap in the onboarding of new employees and developed a new hire development kit.

6. **How would your co-workers describe you?**

    Basically, think of adjectives you honestly feel your co-workers/friends would use to describe you and examples of how the adjectives are supported would be even better. For example: *My co-workers would say I'm very punctual because I'm always the first to work and also I am attentive, thus I frequently facilitate meetings.*

7. **Tell me about a situation in which you had a conflict with another employee and how you handled it.**

    Conflict is unavoidable, but the key is to illustrate how you conducted yourself. Perhaps there was a simple miscommunication issue between you and a co-worker in which you scheduled a meeting with a detailed agenda about the issues needing to be resolved.

8. **Why do you think you will be a good fit for this position?**

    By now you should know why you are great for this position. You can pick out key responsibilities on your resume and give examples of how you performed those job duties successfully in the past. You should list at least four topics with the appropriate level of detail. For example, if you say you are organized, give an example of how your organizational skills correlated to a positive experience.

9. **Tell me about yourself.**

This question throws a lot of people off because they are unsure of how much to say. Your best bet is to give a taste of who you are. Start off with your schooling and quickly move on to big accomplishments in your work life. You don't have to give every single detail about every single job, but rather discuss your higher level experiences. Make sure you pay attention to non-verbal cues as well such as watching the interviewer's face, especially his or her eyes; if they are starting to glaze over, then either move on to the next exciting fact of your life or begin to wrap up. Remember to end the description with how interested you are to work for company XY and how you feel your background fits in perfectly with the company's strategic direction and values.

10. **How much are you asking for compensation?**

You have already done your research on compensation so you should have a good idea how much you deserve for this position. At the beginning interview stages, I generally like to stay away from any talk of money, but if the interviewer presses on for a number, then give a range of the amount you really want; for example, if you are looking for a $60k salary you might say $55-70 thousand. This allots for you to be compensated properly. Remember use payscale.com, glassdoor.com, or salary.com to conduct your research on salary per position.

10 Questions You Can Ask

1. Where do you see this role in two years?

2. What are some of the pain points this position is trying to fill? (In other words, why is this position necessary? If you can get the recruiter to describe the pain points, then you can research and develop a high-level solution for how you would solve their pain.)

3. How long have you worked at XY company?

4. What values and principles do you like about working at XY Company?

5. Is this a brand new position or was there someone else in this role before me?

6. Is there a specific work culture in the office?

7. How does the company measure success?

8. What does the company expect from me in the next 2 months, 6 months, year?

9. How does this position fit into the company road map?

10. Google the company and see the latest current event that is happening, then frame that event into a question that relates to your position or interest about the company.

For example:

You researched Net Suite Inc., which announced an agreement with Dun & Bradstreet. The agreement was to provide NetSuite customers direct access from within its cloud-based business management suite.

The question you could formulate could be, "How is the department estimating the capacity of users from the new NetSuite customers?"

The Interviews

If the interview is face-to-face at a company facility, make sure you print out the directions ahead of time and give yourself plenty of time to reach the location. I would advise leaving your place at least two hours in advance to provide a cushion in case there is traffic and also time to park. If you can, go to the location of the interview the night before to ensure comfort on the day of the interview as well as having a frame of reference for the location.

Moreover, I like to develop an interview prep sheet which contains everything needed to know about the interview, place, time, a snapshot of company data, the questions you will be asked, and even a snapshot of the job description. For a sample of the interview prep sheet, please see Appendix A.

The interview will start the minute you drive into the company's parking lot. You don't know whom you will pass by or who is watching you so always be professional; if you engage in conversation with anyone, make sure you are always positive and friendly. Similarly, the interview is not over until you are down the street from the company parking lot. Doing a happy dance in the company parking lot could backfire, so wait until you are completely off the property.

The Phone Screen

If the initial interview is a phone interview, make sure you find a quiet place with good cell coverage. Remember to have your phone bill paid on the day of your interview. There is nothing more disappointing or embarrassing than having your service disconnected when expecting a call from a potential employer.

The phone screen is used to filter out candidates without the skills and abilities a particular company is seeking. This is your time to articulate your experience and highlight your major accomplishments. On a phone interview, make sure your voice is animated, smooth, and crisp; since the interviewer cannot see your expressions, he or she is relying completely on your voice pitch, tone, and cadence. I recommend dressing in the same manner as you would to a face-to-face interview. This will help settle you into a serious, deliberate mindset. You also should stand during the phone interview. Studies have shown that when people stand, blood is able to flow more easily to the brain, adding agility and quickness to mental functioning.

The One-on-one or Face-to-face

This is pretty self-explanatory and is the traditional form of interviewing. A candidate first meets with an interviewer at the company's location and then may subsequently meet with multiple interviewers. For introverts, this is the preferred interview type because you are only dealing with one person asking questions at a time.

The Panel Interview

The panel interview consists of multiple interviewers (anywhere from 3 to 7) asking you questions individually. This style of interviewing can be intimidating because, with multiple people there, you tend to feel like a fish in a bowl with challenges coming from many directions. Just remain confident and sit up straight. A trick I like to use in an intimidating situation is to press your hands together with the tips of your fingers pressing against each other. For some reason, this calms my nerves and also gives a great impression to others you are in control.

The Skype Interview

The Skype interview is the latest craze. After a phone interview, the next interview could be using the Skype video conference software. Skype saves time because the interviewer doesn't have to be in the same vicinity as you or even the same state. The interviewer still can see what you look like and how you move and respond. To prepare for a Skype interview, make sure you are dressed professionally and the background is clear and free of any distractions, such as rock posters, dirty dishes, or just loud colors. Treat this interview like a face-to-face and remember to smile.

During the Interview

Always provide copies of your resume even if the recruiter says he or she will provide one directly to the interviewer. Things happen and you have to positively swing things in your favor.

Be able to provide details and very specific answers about your experience and how it relates to the position, but don't ramble and check in with the interviewer by saying things like: "Is that clear?" or "Shall I elaborate further?" Always demonstrate a positive can-do attitude; avoid any responses that could be perceived as negative. Be a good listener and refrain from talking over the interviewer or interrupting him or her.

Try to build a rapport with your interviewer. Ask him or her how long he/she has been with the company, what does he/she like about working for the company, etc. Express enthusiasm and interest in the role and the company. Near the end of the interview, after you've demonstrated your experience and learned more about the role, ask whether he/she has any concerns about your ability to perform the job functions and address each concern in a positive and professional manner.

The key is to sell yourself; this is your time to shine. Don't wait for the interviewer to ask the right question. Volunteer extra information that demonstrates your strengths as they relate to the questions asked. The goal is to win so when you think you have given just enough, give more. This strategy is a delicate dance, however, because you don't want to be arrogant or even desperate, but rather passionate and thorough. As the interview comes to a close, don't ask for the job. Instead, inquire about the next steps in the process and gently offer to present samples of your work.

Always Provide Samples of Your Work

It is critical to do more than just pat yourself on the back repeatedly during the interview. You must back it up with proof and it is best to have more at your disposal than just telling anecdotes. If you can, bring along samples of your work in a PowerPoint presentation, an Excel spreadsheet, or an artwork portfolio. The key is to show something you created or accomplished, while demonstrating your ability to communicate information effectively.

Give the interviewer your job description matrix that was discussed earlier. Not only does this show strategic initiative to your interviewer, it also can make their job easier if they need to sell your candidacy to their managers.

During the Final Interview

If you are successful enough to make it to the final interview, you should develop an action plan—maybe a 30- to 60-day action plan addressing some of the challenges/pain points the manager has that you discussed in the initial interviews. This can be an incredibly powerful example of how focused and strategic you will be as a potential employee.

Thank You Letters

After the interview, remember to send a follow-up thank you letter—the sooner the better. Remember, you want to thank each of the interviewers for his or her time and again restate all the experience and skills you discussed during the interview. For examples of thank you letters, please see Appendix F.

KEY POINTS TO REMEMBER

- **Do your research** on the company. Use Google to dig into the company and visit its website.

- **Do your research** on the interviewer. Use LinkedIn, Facebook, and/or Google.

- **Make sure** you have concrete examples of how you have achieved success in the past.

- **Prepare** for the type of interview you are going to attend with focus and confidence.

- **Offer** to give examples/samples of your past work.

- If possible, **create** an action plan for how you would address the manager's pressing issues once you started work with the firm.

- **Send** a thank you letter ASAP.

CHAPTER **12**

THE WAITING GAME: REASONS WHY YOU DIDN'T GET A SECOND INTERVIEW

Patience is not simply the ability to wait - it's how we behave while we're waiting.

– JOYCE MEYER

A NY GOOD INTERVIEW can feel similar to a romantic date you swore went so well—it automatically guarantees a second. Unfortunately, as the days drift by, your mind begins to question why there hasn't been any contact to solidify the next engagement. Listed below are 20 potential reasons why the company/interviewer completely disappeared. Please keep in mind you should never take the company's lack of communication as a personal affront; it just simply was not meant to be.

1. **You weren't the right gender:** The employer really had a woman/man envisioned for the role. Of course, they can't legally share that information with you.

2. **You fell just short**: You had 95 percent of what they were looking for, but that last 5 percent was a deal-breaker.

That last 5 percent could be five years of experience you simple don't have.

3. **An inside job:** They already had someone in mind for the role, but there is a company policy to post the position.

4. **Just fishing:** The company is just testing the waters and has no intention of hiring anyone for the position at the moment.

5. **Insecurity:** Your intelligence was threatening to the interviewer. Believe it or not, there are hiring managers who are insecure and worry that a new person could come in and threaten his or her job.

6. **You weren't the right race**: Racism/racial bias does exist; it's just hard to prove. Your race may not be the right image for the company. People who look like you may have performed poorly in the past and the company is not willing to take another chance with you.

7. **You are too old**: Ageism is alive and prevalent. If you are over the age of 40, your experience needs to display a boatload of success. Your competition is younger talent with knowledge of the latest technology and who are willing to be paid a lot less.

8. **You are too young**: Employers may not believe you can handle the responsibilities of the job based on their experiences with younger employees in the past. Unfortunately, that is a bias and has nothing to do with your skills.

9. **You stayed too long at your last job:** Years ago, this was a given; you remained with a job for at least a decade. Anything less and future employers would wonder what is wrong with you. Now, if you stay longer than five years in your last position, employers wonder whether you are current with the latest technology.

10. **You didn't stay long enough at your last job**: Looks are everything and they may wonder when you're trying

to explain why you left your last job after less than six months. Be honest, but don't volunteer unnecessary information either.

11. **Culture fit**: They didn't believe you would fit in with the culture. Again, are you in the majority or the minority and are there younger employees than you or older ones? Did most of the employees go to ultra-prestigious schools? Again, the reason could be a hidden bias. You may never know, so move on and don't spend the energy dwelling.

12. **Your dress was too casual:** I always suggest you play to win and wear your Sunday best – this is absolutely basic, yet necessary.

13. **Your resume was solid, but you didn't "wow" anyone:** I know all the work you've done in the past has been amazing and meaningful to you, but if that is not clearly displayed on your resume, then you will be overlooked in a pool of hundreds of applicants.

14. **The budget for the position was cut:** Due to a change in direction from management, this position is no longer needed.

15. **They didn't like the tie you wore:** This is here because the reason they didn't choose you could come down to something as insignificant as the color of your tie or the length of your skirt. Don't take it personally.

16. **You were asking for too much money:** You should have an idea of how much the position will pay; often it is displayed in the posting. You should know what you're worth based on the amount of experience you've had in your field. Don't ever talk about money until the interviewer has made you an offer.

17. **You weren't asking for enough money:** They had a number in mind they were willing to pay for the position; however, you mentioned a figure much less than they were going to pay, thus they are starting to suspect your qualifications.

18. **Your references were lackluster:** Your references did not hype you up. Please only use people in your life who want to see you succeed. Ask them directly: "Will you give me a good reference?" If they hesitate, even a second, don't place their name on your resume.

19. **You lied on your resume:** They found out you lied on your resume about a school, a job, or a credential and they put your file in the shredder.

20. **Bad luck:** They found someone else at the last minute through a referral.

KEY POINTS TO REMEMBER

- Hiring managers will be graded on how well they hired thus, they will pay extra attention to the potential employee they want to hire.

- Ideally, the goal should be to have multiple job interviews in a given period of time so you don't have all your eggs in one basket.

- Don't take it personally if you never get a call or email back. Just continue with your search, revising your resume often, polishing your 30-second elevator speech, and networking with new people.

CHAPTER **13**

DEPRESSION DOESN'T LIVE HERE

It's so easy for me to fall back into depression. I think it comes with having money. I don't have to work. I could be sitting bored and depressed at home with a bag on my head.

– KELLY OSBOURNE

A LOT OF the suggestions mentioned earlier about keeping active were meant to prevent falling into a depressive or discouraged state. This chapter discusses how to get out of that depressive state if you did fall into it. Some of the techniques listed here helped me snap out of my pity party and get back to living life with purpose and passion.

During your job search, there will be times when you get discouraged and even depressed. You will have good days when you feel extremely productive and you will have bad days when rolling out of bed is a struggle. Be aware of the negative thoughts that creep into the mind and whisper, "You'll never be successful again" or "You don't deserve to win." These thoughts can creep in when you least expect them and knock you down. Please, please ignore these thoughts! It's just your mind playing games with you, in a weird way just trying to keep you safe. Due to the way the mind works, it is critical for you to have a plan for keeping yourself grounded and keeping a balanced perspective on your life. Below is a snapshot of how I felt after I left my job of six years.

Some days I would wake up and sit in bed staring at the ceiling. Who am I? Is this my life? What the hell am I doing with my life? I just can't believe this is the life that I'm living! Where, oh where, did I go wrong Lord?

I couldn't help but feel pressure as I drifted closer and closer toward my 33rd birthday. What had I done with my life? What major accomplishments had I achieved? My brother is married with THREE kids! Hell, I'd be lucky to find someone to go to the movies with on a Friday night.

How many more interviews do I need to go on before I get an offer? I've been on ten interviews in the last 3 months and the feedback I consistently hear is they are looking for someone with more experience. Ugh!

When I'm feeling down or sinking into a pity party, I have a few techniques that help me snap back to a more positive state of being.

- **Listen to Old Music**: When I say old music, I mean music you used to listen to in grade school or listened to when you felt safe and understood. Music has a way of transporting you back to that time and place, a time when you felt encouraged about the future and awe-struck about life.

- **Write out and speak positive affirmations**: What are affirmations? They are simply positive statements that affirm whatever it is you want. For example, I like to use the affirmation: "I am open and receptive to receiving all the good that God has for me."

  This affirmation reinforces the thought that I will be in the position to receive good things. I sometimes feel I sabotage the good things from happening to me in life so I like saying this affirmation to counteract the negativity. To learn more about affirmations and to hear new ones, check out Louise Hay on her YouTube channel:

▶ https://www.youtube.com/watch?v=olI9ocFpTyY

▶ https://www.youtube.com/watch?v=Deop3NybMDQ

- **Get social:** Talk to friends and family and reminisce about past successes.

- **Occupy your mind:** Watch a favorite movie from the past or re-read a favorite book.

- **Go for Therapy:** I know therapy can be expensive and may not be covered well under your budget healthcare plan; however, numerous government agencies and some non-profit groups provide free counseling, so look for those opportunities as well. A few sessions with a professional may work wonders in terms of providing support and techniques you need to break out of a serious funk. Another option is to seek a therapist on groupon.com, living social, or even Amazon local. Type in therapist or counseling and see what is available in your neck of the woods.

Please note: I knew if I ever stayed in bed longer than three days something was wrong and I needed to do something drastic. I am not a therapist, but if you have no desire to get out of bed after three days, please call somebody immediately.

Time to get Spiritual

- **Go to church or synagogue:** Explore all of the services in your local church community. They may have a wide range of resources to support you on your quest.

- **Post a YouTube video:** I'm sure there are at least one or two things you know how to do really well that you would be able to convey to the world. By producing something new, you will change your mindset from being a consumer to being a producer. It will give your mindset a whole new perspective and it is incredibly fun.

- **Get positive vibes:** Listen to positive affirmations at night and wake up refreshed and ready to tackle the day.

- **Start meditation:** Meditation is a practice that involves self-regulating the mind. Meditation is used to clear the mind of thoughts and may ease high blood pressure and relieve depression and anxiety. Meditation is usually done by sitting alone in a quiet place and breathing in and out to various rhythmic patterns.

  Many people find meditation can be done with special music in the background or in silence.

  There are a host of videos that provide meditations on YouTube, at your local library, and on Amazon to purchase. Check out the guided meditations below. I recommend you begin with a perennial favorite such as Louise Hay.

▶ https://www.youtube.com/watch?v=4jNV1FV-_Os

▶ https://www.youtube.com/watch?v=2uTuztdcKvs

KEY POINTS TO REMEMBER

- **Reflect** on past success and remember how it made you feel.

- **Get some therapy**; talk to someone every week, maybe even more.

- **Write** out positive affirmations and then stick them on your wall all around your residence.

- **Recite** positive affirmations.

- **Try meditation.**

- **Check out** YouTube videos on dealing with depression.

CHAPTER **14**

WHEN ALL HELL BREAKS LOOSE

If you're going through hell, keep going.

– WINSTON CHURCHILL

I T'S BEEN SIX months and you still haven't found an opportunity that resonates with what you're seeking. You've sent out countless resumes, applied online for more than 50 positions, and you've gone on more than 10 interviews—and no one's even called you back. You have a positive attitude, but the reality is your bank account is really starting to drain. Not only are the bills adding up, but extra expenses just keep showing up as well. It's like all hell is breaking loose. What do you do?

You are in a negative spiral and you have to break it immediately.

Pray

No matter what your spiritual or religious beliefs, anyone can give thanks and ask for something from a higher power. At this time, you need to pray like you have never prayed before. Let God or the Universe or whomever or whatever you believe in hear you and give all Glory and Honor to him for the trials and tribulations you are experiencing. You can look at this situation as a test or look at it as an opportunity that will build your character. Regardless, just take a moment to surrender yourself to something much bigger than you.

Take Each Opportunity One at a Time

Don't focus on the debt or the bill collectors calling you or how you are going to pay your rent in two weeks. Just focus on what you can do today and tomorrow you can focus on the rent. Life has a way of opening up and surprising you when you least expect it, but if everything starts coming at you at once, you may feel over-whelmed. You need to be strong and resist the temptation to slide into a depressive state of mind.

Schedule the Bills Out

Many times if you call up your credit card company, insurance provider, or even your cell phone provider, and provide them a future payment date, then they won't cancel your service. Make a partial payment and then work out an arrangement for the rest. The goal is to give yourself more time to pay, so schedule the date for at least two weeks in the future.

Activate Plan C

In Chapter 3, we discussed having a backup plan when things go poorly. If you are at that point now, then activate plan C.

It was on a Monday and multiple debit card transactions were hitting my checking account. I forgot to call the individual companies and stop the automatic payment before they hit the account. It was like there was no end in sight! For every hit, there was a $33 overdraft fee and the hits just kept coming and the fees were adding up. I had racked up over $180 in fees, not to mention the original charge to the account. I made calls to the customer service department and spoke with different customer service reps, praying they would help me in this situation. I just wanted some help, some understanding, some compassion—I received none. I needed a break, some kind of relief, so I got down on my knees and prayed. I prayed like I never prayed before. I finally decided to go into a bank branch and talk to someone face-to-face. I talked to one of the branch managers and he reversed several fees and helped me close out my account. Instantly my life began to change. Other situations began to bear fruit and I knew it was because of God. Whether it was the parking attendant who let me leave because I didn't have cash on me, or the electric company sending me a refund check in the mail so I could stop worrying about how I was going to pay for gas to get to my temp job the next day, I knew no matter how hard I tried to deny it – or simply not believe it – GOD just kept showing up.

KEY POINTS TO REMEMBER

- **Pray** like you have never prayed before. Prayer does work!

- Make sure you are **aware** of all the bills automatically debited from your account. If necessary, call the companies in advance and cancel the automatic payments.

- Take it **one issue at a time**. Don't focus on all the "bad" things happening. That will only bring in more bad things.

- **Make** a partial payment and schedule the bills out

- **Activate** Plan C.

CHAPTER **15**

12 WAYS TO SAVE/MAKE MONEY INSTANTLY

The lack of money is the root of all evil.

MARK TWAIN

WHILE YOU'RE ON the job search, there will be many times when you will need some fast cash. Listed below are some quick ideas for receiving some immediate cash.

- **Redeem points on a credit or debit card**: Remember when you were working and went shopping for a new wardrobe? Well, you probably racked up some points on your card. Research the number of points and see if you can redeem the points for a gift card at a store where you shop for necessary items such as groceries or gas.

- **Check in the couch, under the couch, very crevice you can find**: Look in the car, under the seats, between the seats, and in the trunk. You may be surprised by how many coins have disappeared into the tiniest cracks.

- **Sign up for focus groups**: This is a great way to make some good easy money. You could earn between $50 and $200, give or take. It really just depends on the topic, which can range from new technologies to your favorite bar of soap. Simply go to focusgroup.com and enter in your demographic information. There may be a series of questions for you to answer. If you qualify for the study, or the focus group, someone will call and schedule an appointment for you to show up at a specific location.

- **Sign up as an extra for TV or film:** Believe it or not, Hollywood isn't just in Hollywood, California anymore. A lot of production companies have found it more cost-effective to produce TV and films outside of California. These production companies are always looking for real people to fill in the background, to give the scene more texture and realism. Background acting opportunities can last a couple of hours or a couple of days. The pay can vary from $50 to $250 a day if you are non-union, but members of SAG-AFTRA, you can make 3 to 4 times the previous amount depending on the project. Thus regardless of where you live, see if there are any productions taking place in your area. **Boost your borrowing**: Before you leave your job officially, request an increase in your credit limit so you have some backup room for emergencies. Try to do this with as many credit cards as you have, but don't abuse the credit cards. Debt should only be used for emergencies and/or essentials, perhaps when your car breaks down. Anything can happen and having a credit card to take care of these unexpected expenses is a lifesaver.

- **Get creative:** Don't pay $8 to $10 a month for phone insurance. Many credit card companies offer benefits like insurance for people whom regularly pay phone bills using a credit card. Call your credit card company and ask if they have such a program. This way, if you then lose your phone, the deductible for a replacement is either negligible or nonexistent.

- **Scale down:** Cut out the cable bill or anything you know can be found on the Internet.

- **Try looking for a loan at reputable places:** Try a company called Nix.com for cash. They are funded by a Kinetica Credit Union whose mission is to help people get out of debt, not continue to spiral into it (https://www.kinecta.org/locations/).

- **Recycle:** Start collecting cans and glass and plastic bottles. After a couple of months and three garbage bags full of recyclables, you could be looking at anywhere from $5-$15. I know it's not much, but this amount is perfect to pay for laundry every month. Plus, recycling is good for the environment, so it's a win/win. Don't forget to ask other friends or family members for their recyclables as well; this will boost your profit and help them keep their garage cleaner.

- **Return:** Look in your closet and see if you can return anything you really just don't need, even if it's slightly used. Most stores like Wal-Mart, Target, Best Buy, or even Macy's have policies allowing the return of an item with the receipt, even if it has been opened, unless its electronic. So don't be afraid to just ask someone at customer service ahead of time if you can return something, but do your research.

- **Redeem gift cards:** Do you have leftover gift cards you really just can't use? There are sites, like giftcard.com, where you can submit your gift cards and they will send you a check in about two weeks, minus a percentage based on the amount. For more of an immediate need, you can also submit a gift card to your local Payday loan store or some gold stores. At these stores the percentage is so high that it's practically like giving up half the value of the gift card to get the cash.

- **Find small jobs:** You might want to look into the on-demand jobs that are growing right now. From Uber and Lyft to Postmates and Jolt, a whole new assortment of jobs are available for anyone with a clean driving record and a relatively new smartphone. In Chapter 16, I discuss my own personal experiences with these services and how much money can be made.

KEY POINTS TO REMEMBER

- **Increase** your credit limits before you are officially in-between jobs.

- **Be frugal.** Now is not the time to go shopping for new clothes or electronic gear. You are on a strict budget, so act like it.

- **Cash out** those credit card points.

- **Recycle** cans, plastic, and glass for cash.

- Only drive when you have to; **walk more.**

- **Be creative** and find new ways to save. Look for YouTube tips on ways to save money posted by other savers.

- **Use coupons.**

- **Cut** that cable cord.

CHAPTER **16**

THE ON-DEMAND ECONOMY

*What new technology does is create new opportunities to do
a job that customers want done.*

– TIM O'REILLY

Technology has surged forward exponentially within the last five years. There are apps for practically anything, which means there are more opportunities to work for companies that developed and support these applications.

Due to an increased need for some quick cash flow, I decided to try out Uber and Jolt.com. I heard about Uber, but I never thought I would be driving for them. I came up with every excuse in the book about why I would never drive for them. I mean, I was a college graduate with over 10 years of project management experience—I was not *that* desperate. Actually, it's only beneath you until you are out of money and everywhere you look a door is slamming in your face. It is very humbling how suddenly your perspective changes when your bank account balance resembles your monthly cell phone bill.

Uber Driving

Aside from taxi drivers and shuttle companies that have been accused of over-charging consumers and forcing them to accept their brand of questionable customer service and inadequate levels of personal hygiene, just about everyone else appreciates this new option for traveling cheaper and, in some cases, in style.

I'll never forget my first ride using Uber in Los Angeles. I was travelling from the LAX Airport to my home in Culver City. The Uber driver, an actor making some money in between auditions, had a brand-new Mazda. As he drove to my destination, we chatted about art and being creative. I was amazed at how fast you could build a rapport with a stranger with just a few lines of communication. After I was dropped off, I was hooked with this service and realized from that moment on my future mode of transportation would never be the same.

Obviously, the biggest questions are whether you really can make money, can avoid picking up some unusual characters, and how far you need to drive. Take a look at the sections below that address many of the questions that I had entering this new endeavor.

The Pay

Your pay rate depends on when you start with the company. Those who joined the company before October 2015 keep about 80 percent of the cost of a trip. Others who joined the company later are keeping about 75 percent of each trip. Keep in mind that Uber and Lyft are constantly evolving and adjusting to the market as well as the laws of the region or country they operate in.

To make more money with Uber, you need to drive when the demand is high. For Uber, that means when demand is surging, the normal cost is multiplied by 1.2X, 1.3X, 2.6X, etc.

The most profitable times are on the weekends, which start at 5 p.m. on Fridays until 2 a.m. on Monday morning. Some of the most profitable drives are club pick-ups, airport pick-ups, and hotel pick-ups. The other profitable times are during the holidays, especially the Fourth of July, Thanksgiving, Christmas, and New Year's Eve. I haven't seen statistics, but Halloween seems to be getting bigger and bigger every year, especially in the state of California. I would highly suggest driving on all major holidays.

The People

Uber and Lyft users come from all walks of life—business travelers to broke teenagers who are excited to be able to take their girl/guy out on a date for the first time. The people can be extremely nice, offering plenty of conversation the whole ride or hardly letting on that they are there. I loved it when passengers would talk because it was like I was taking a friend to the airport or giving them a ride home, but getting paid for it.

My Style

I wanted to project an air of confidence and professionalism, so I made a decision that every time I drove I would have my car freshly clean and would wear a dress shirt and tie. I liked to establish a minimum of decorum of professionalism, which also helps me to get into the space I am working since I'm not just giving a friend a ride. I would also do a cursory check of the backseat and would wipe the leather down with leather cleaner to make the car extra crisp. The driving experience really depends on what part of the world you live in and where you drive. I was nervous before my first trip for Uber. I sat in the car and prepared my mind before I started the engine wondering if I would be smart enough to use the app or take directions from the driver and appear I had everything under control. Everyone is different, especially with directions, but since you are being paid for your service, utilize the applications Uber provides.

The Driving

I drove in L.A. The benefits of driving in a place like Beverly Hills is the trip takes longer and the demand is higher, so the rate for the trip is higher also.

Driving for a Food Delivery Service

After driving for Uber, I wanted to continue to be open to additional money-producing opportunities. While driving for Uber, I met a man who introduced me to a food delivery service, Jolt. The benefit of this work, unlike driving people around, is there is the amount of tips you may receive.

Much like Uber, the communication was through an app on your phone. The app would alert you to a restaurant where you would pick up an order. The goal, of course, was to be close to your delivery destination so you could get there quickly and get a great tip. Sometimes however, the company was short on drivers and every order was behind causing customers to wait longer than they felt they should and my tip would suffer.

I delivered food in L.A. from Santa Monica to West Hollywood and from Brentwood to UCLA. Each delivery is different, but there are two deliveries that really stood out for me.

The Brentwood Delivery

It was 9:30 p.m. and traffic was thick as I was heading to a place in Brentwood. The ticket had already been paid for with a credit card and a $4 tip was already included. As I entered the neighborhood, it was almost eerily quiet. Light fixtures lined the street and created a fairyland atmosphere. I arrived at the address and parked my car a little way down the street. As I walked toward the house,

I thought to myself, "This is how the rich live. This is absolutely beautiful." I arrived at the door, rang the bell, and then knocked. A pleasant Caucasian woman arrived and I gave her the food. She called to her husband to pay me and when he arrived he asked if the traffic was heavy. I told him yes and apologized for the delay. He handed me a wad of cash and in return I gave him the receipt. A second later, he asked if he could have three dollars back. I said OK, not even realizing how much was in my hand. I dug in my pocket to get some ones and had none. I looked to see how much he gave and it was two twenties. I said I didn't have ones, but I'd give him a five. He looked disappointed, but just turned and said to just keep the change and closed the door. In a bit of a stupor, I said thank you, turned, and left. Why was he so generous I thought? Did he know of my plight? I dare not question the blessing anymore and I just accepted it as a direct blessing from God.

The Lexington International Delivery

Yes, I was now delivering barbecue to the same company I had worked for as a project manager for six years. Luckily, the location was not the one where I worked, so I wasn't worried in the least about running into someone familiar. All I can say is delivering that barbecue took about 35 minutes from the time I picked up the food to the time I set it out on the table for the doctors. I walked away with a $45 tip, easy money I thought.

Working for Uber and Jolt filled a need when money was in demand for me while I was changing jobs. The bottom line is: if you want to make extra money, then you have to drive. If you do so, you will get paid every week (usually on a Thursday). The money will be deposited directly into your bank account. A word of caution if you plan to do work for Lyft, Uber, or any part of the on-demand economy, be aware you will put miles and wear/tear on your car, so be prepared to expense everything you can on your taxes.

KEY POINTS TO REMEMBER

- Don't be surprised if you find yourself humbled due to circumstance.

- Don't be afraid to **try new things**.

- The **on-demand economy** is great for extra money, especially if you are a people person.

- The pay can be good if you take advantage of the late night party crowd and holidays.

- **Don't limit yourself!** Maximize all opportunities when meeting new people.

- If you plan to be a driver, be aware you will put miles and wear/tear on your car.

CONCLUSION

CELEBRATE

Don't let the fear of the time it will take to accomplish
something stand in the way of your doing it. The time will
pass anyway; we might just as well put that passing time to
the best possible use.

– EARL NIGHTINGALE

A JOB SEARCH can be very frustrating and, with technology changing so rapidly now, traditional methods that were the standard are no longer applicable. But change will always be the rule, whether it's 2016 or 2060. Changes will always be present; how we adapt and use that change to our advantage is key.

A job search is not a pleasant experience. It is full of rejection and it can even lead you down several rabbit holes. Nevertheless, being unemployed gives you time to reflect on your life and truly determine what is most important to you.

In the process, we draw a clearer picture of what we want out of life and the style of work we feel most comfortable doing. It comes with an opportunity to learn new skills, time to write that book you have been procrastinating about for years, more time to spend with your children, time to spend with your mother or father, or even time to learn how to get in better shape by going to the gym.

Another point about unemployment is it forces you to look at yourself objectively. You have to constantly examine your strengths and weaknesses. If you don't like what you find, then take the time to improve them. The key is to learn how to package your skills and abilities to market them in a most appealing way to someone who will be willing to hire you. You do this by understanding the trends and what other candidates are doing, and then do it better.

My ascension back to re-employment came through networking with a family member who knew of an open position in his own company. Due to my background, I was able to slide into the position.

I'll never forget prepping for the interview. I was told I would be interviewing with five people via the Internet, probably using Skype. When the day came, I was ready; I researched each person using LinkedIn and Facebook, plus my contact at the company gave me some inside tips. I wore a great outfit—a three-piece suit—and I made sure the lighting for my laptop camera was appealing. I even rearranged pictures on my wall in the background to reflect awards and plaques I received over the years. Needless to say, I was playing to win. When the interview began, I came out the gate swinging by answering their questions with a lot of energy and confidence.

The interview was on a Friday and I thought it went well. When I called the internal recruiter on Monday morning, he asked me how I thought I did. I replied I thought it really went well and I would certainly like the opportunity to work for a team like Solar Industries. I said I believed I could contribute a great deal and felt we could do great things together. He told me they felt the same way and I would be an asset to the team.

Before I had time to even send out a thank you letter, I was already offered the job. I was extremely excited. Finally, I had found a permanent job that would pay me more money for my skills and abilities than I ever made in the tech industries. The company had been around for several years in the tech industry and I soon learned their culture was very similar to a start-up culture. So now, all that was left for me to do was to celebrate.

When you discover your next job or opportunity, you will celebrate also. Listed below are some suggestions. Go out and live it up—you deserve it!

- Get a massage and relax in luxury.
- Go to the movies.
- Go to an ice-cream parlor and get the works.
- Get a manicure or pedicure.
- Go to the mall and buy a new outfit.
- Go out to a dance club with your best friends and buy a round of drinks for everybody.
- Bake a cake and eat the whole thing.

Whatever you decide, do something! You've worked hard and you deserve to celebrate your success.

So what have you learned? To survive your job search you have to balance several activities from keeping fit to creating a professional online presence; every day you must be actively engaged on your goal. Also, you've learned networking is everything in the 21st century. People hire people they know, they trust, and who most look like them. The truth is networking is done best when there is a story involved, a connection between two people with no strings attached.

I hope you will take the time to follow some of the methods, tips, and tricks in this book and fill your "in-between time" with joy and laughter. Pretty soon, even really soon, you will receive the type of job or opportunity that is most rewarding and meaningful to you. Your next opportunity is on its way to bringing you closer and closer to your amazing destiny.

REFERENCES

Web links

http://www.brainyquote.com/quotes/topics/topic_work.html#TqwHcZzPYFCi2Ufc.99

http://insights.dice.com/2015/08/28/surviving-the-final-interview/

https://en.wikipedia.org/wiki/Meditation

http://www.businessinsider.com/signs-you-should-quit-your-job-2016-2/#-9

http://www.businesspundit.com/20-best-jobs-for-introverts-04-2016/4/

Books

- *The 4 Year Work Week* - Tim Ferris
- *Escape From Corporate America* – Pamela Skillings
- *Unemployed But Moving On!* – Cherly Butler Long
- *Career Comeback* – Bradley G. Richardson

Appendixes

Appendix A

Listed below is an Interview Prep Sheet, which I created to utilize before every interview. This document contains a list of critical interview information for maximum preparedness. *The information under each title is an example; fill in each description to fit your interview needs.*

Description of Company Division

The Group's Digital Media team is responsible for developing ancillary digital revenue streams for Television Group's diverse portfolio of broadcast and cable networks. This includes product development, marketing and operations for the Group's digital media content platforms. The team has been at the forefront of many of the company's pioneering technical innovations, including being the first network to offer full episodes in 2005 to the recent deployment of its industry defining WATCH services, which made the Television Group the first to provide authenticated users access to both live, 24/7 linear network streams as well as an extensive offering of advantaged window on demand episodes on desktops, connected TVs, smartphones and tablets.

The Overall Job Description

The Program Manager will be responsible for the day-to-day oversight, communication, scheduling, and budgeting of digital initiatives for Digital Media. This position requires proven project management experience (including prioritizing, estimating, scheduling, budgeting and resourcing multiple projects and cross-functional teams) and familiarity with digital technologies. Successful candidates must be proactive, detail-oriented, and able to clearly communicate tasks, schedules, dependencies, risks, issues, and processes to a variety of business, creative, and technical audiences.

The Date and Time of the Interview

Tuesday, June 16th @ 4pm PST – Please arrive no later than 3:45 p.m. to allow time for parking. I will meet you there with resumes in hand. If you need anything, my number is (xxx) xxx-6800.

The Location of the Interview

Where: 3800 W Alameda Ave., xxxx, CA. Park in the visitor's parking lot. I will meet you in front of Starbucks at the long tables.

Attire: Business Professional (Suit jacket, pants, dress shirt, and polished shoes)

Specific Department

Who: XXX Media Technology & Strategy Group, Program Manager – Jane Doe -LinkedIn Profile attached:

Link to Company Website:

Specific Job Duties and Responsibilities

- Successful administration and support of project management systems, tools, processes, and templates
- Possesses a level of maturity, emotional intelligence and the ability to thrive in a complex and dynamic environment

- Supports creation, maintenance, and distribution of all P3MO reports for the Leadership Team

- Encourages prompt time tracking by project team members in support of the Finance Team

- Anticipates the needs of project, program, and P3MO management; makes independent decisions and takes action to meet those needs

- Displays independent evaluation and judgment required for handling a wide variety of situations and for taking appropriate action while maintaining a high level of professionalism and confidentiality

- Assists in the effective tracking and communication of project status

- Assists in the accurate and thorough entry and set up of projects and programs in MS Project Server

- Assists in the accurate and thorough archival of project documentation in SharePoint

- Acts as a reference point for P3MO queries and information, and an advocate for best practices in project management

- Assists Program and Project Managers with use of MS Project Server, ensuring data is entered accurately and thoroughly

- Assists with lessons learned, best practices and project closure

Job Requirements

KNOWLEDGE, SKILLS, AND ABILITIES

- B.S. or B.A. in related field
- PMP certification a plus

- Minimum of two to five years of solid PMO Project Analyst, Project Coordinator, or Project Administrator experience, and working knowledge of the project management discipline

- Project Management experience a plus

- Full understanding and working experience with Microsoft Project and Project Web App (PWA) 2010/2013

- Experienced user of MS Office (Outlook, Word, Excel, and PowerPoint)

- Excellent verbal and written communication to ask for help

- Ability to make intuitive decisions, prioritize, and multi-task (i.e. manage multiple tasks and cope with ever changing priorities); also knows when to escalate

- Experience working in a fast-paced environment with changing needs

Appendix B

Sample Cover Letter 1

Your Name
Your address
Your email

Company Name
300 W Ocean Blvd #13
Santa Monica, CA90802, USA

Greetings Company X,

The opportunity to work for a dynamic, fast-paced, innovative gaming organization is incredibly exciting. As a Senior Project Coordinator, my professional background demonstrates superior achievements; I am confident I will excel in the position of Project Coordinator. I have brought much success to my past employers and I know I can bring similar success to Cie Games.

I consistently use my creativity to create PowerPoint presentations, detailed Visio diagrams, and numerous Excel spreadsheets to effectively communicate business ideas and objectives to executive management. I have enclosed my resume to provide a summary of my qualifications and background for your review.

I am positioned to exceed your expectations. I have excellent communication skills, an outstanding work ethic, and the ability to work well in both team-oriented and self-directed environments. I welcome an opportunity to meet with you to discuss my qualifications in further detail in a personal interview. Thank you for your time and I look forward to your response.

Best Regards,

Jared Powell

(xxx) xxx-xxxx

Sample Cover Letter 2

Your Name

Your Address

Your Email

Business Name

Business Address

Date:

To Whom It May Concern:

Currently, I am enrolled at the UCLA Extension School as a student in the Entertainment Studies Certification program and am highly motivated to secure an internship in the industry for the Spring 2012.

I bring to the table a wealth of creative skills cultivated over the course of my employment as a project consultant and manager. I have worked with others to effectively set time frames, schedule meetings, document meeting minutes, and meet the deadline of various project activities.

The enclosed resume provides more details of my skills and achievements. I am positive I will be a great asset to your team. Thank you so much for your time and consideration and I look forward to speaking with you

Best Regards,

Jared Powell

(XXX) XXX-XXXX

Appendix C

Sample Resume 1

Jared C. Powell

(310) 767 – 7935 ◆ San Francisco, CA 94107

Jaredpowell95@gmail.com ◆ linkedin.com/in/jared-c-powell-PMTrainer.

Multi-tooled professional with 8+ years of experience supporting enterprise-level projects, delivering corporate level training, identifying project deliverables, setting project timelines, and providing presentations/reports to executive leadership. I am adept at facilitation between multi-functional departments to reach key business objectives and project milestones.

Education and Certifications

- 2000 B.S., Mechanical Engineering, Tuskegee University, Tuskegee, AL
- 2008 Extension Program, Project Management – University of California, Berkeley CA
- 2009 Project Management Professional – Project Management Institute: San Francisco, CA
- 2015 Certified, Agile Expert Certificate - Scrum Study Institute

Professional Experience

Project Manager/ Corporate Trainer

SolarCity, **San Francisco,CA** **12/2015 – 6/2016**

- Successfully extended the SolarCity brand to Mexico by developing the website SolarCity.mx.
- Trained the Internal SolarCity Marketing Team on internal E-commerce Request Process Flow

- Scheduled/coordinated project kick-off and review meetings. Set agendas, lead meetings, lead calls, identified open questions; Set meeting agendas, captured meeting minutes, and set critical next steps

- Prioritized between 10–25 multiple JIRA tickets for weekly sprints; responsible for backlog grooming of 65 to 75 JIRA tickets per week.

Project Manager/ Corporate Instructor - Contractor
12/2011 – 11/2015

ABSCO Technology, Los Angeles, CA

- Taught PMIs PMP approved curriculum to select group of Denso project managers/supervisors

- Developed daily lesson plans and developed additional instructional material to aid in educational instruction

- Motivated students/project managers to actively participate in all aspects of the educational process

- Provided students with creative exercises to reinforce critical project management skills

Farmer's Insurance, Los Angeles, CA

- Successfully delivered the Graded Death Benefit (GDB) project to the Farmers.com Digital Market

- Placed improved online customer experience and generated a new online revenue stream

- Successfully implemented the three New Life Products to the Farmers Digital Market Place and improved the online customer experience.

- Effectively tested and deployed the UBI code in the Farmer Insurance's Production environment

DirecTV, El Segundo, CA

- Successfully developed a weekly departmental process that identified future dependency needs, mitigated project risks and documented strategies for resolving issues and maximizing lab efficiency

- Facilitated weekly Test Lab Review meetings. Forecasted future project asset/dependency needs, identified project risks and reprioritized projects based on new change requests

- Consolidated multiple work stream status updates into one executive status report using MS Word and PowerPoint

Warner Bros., Burbank, CA

- Created and delivered weekly dashboards and status reports using established project management tools such as Excel and PowerPoint. Tracked resource allocation and forecasted personnel needs for the Contractor Resource Program by creating and managing multiple spreadsheets/workbooks and pivot tables to present to executive-level management

- Created/updated company newsletters regarding new relevant technologies to internal department

- Developed web instructions (specifically for Xbox 360) for Warner Bros. properties (Injustice, CW App, Flixter)

Kaiser Permanente, Oakland, CA and Rancho Cucamonga, CA 1/2006 – 11/2011

Senior Project Coordinator/CCES Program

- Supervised business analysts and consultants to develop business requirements and identify business artifacts

- Collaborated daily with IT Project Manager to implement SDLC methodologies

- Established project timelines for contract configurations, solidified project deliverables (Project Charter, Scope Document,

Action Log, Risk Log), and obtained buy-in from stakeholders

Senior Project Consulting Associate, Revenue Cycle

- Successfully managed/completed large data analysis projects aimed to increase revenues by 10 to 15 million and improve customer service

SAMPLE RESUME 2

JARED POWELL

(310) 767-7935 • 3308 Stone Ridge Avenue
Los Angeles, CA 90032

SENIOR PROJECT COORDINATOR

Results driven professional with demonstrated proficiency in project management, data analysis, report generation, presentation development, and producing complex diagrams. Effective communicator adept at organizing and producing comprehensive project artifacts. Consistently explores opportunities to further elevate customer loyalty and increase revenues.

TECHNICAL SKILLS AND ABILITIES

- Project Management / Coordination
- Strategy Development / Implementation
- CAD Software (Mechanica, AutoCAD)
- Microsoft Office Suite (MS Project, Excel, Visio)
- Data Analysis
- Knowledge of Waterfall and Agile Methodologies

EDUCATION / CERTIFICATIONS

2012 Certificate Candidate (Business and Entertainment Studies), *UCLA*; Los Angeles, CA

2009 Certified Project Management Professional, *Project Management Institute*; San Francisco, CA

2008 Extension Program, Project Management, *UC Berkeley*; Berkeley, CA

2000 Bachelor of Science, Mechanical Engineering, Tuskegee University; Tuskegee, AL

Professional Experience

DirecTv	**El Segundo, CA**	**8/2013 - Present**

Senior Project Coordinator

- Provide weekly updates on Test Lab Projects using Excel spreadsheets and PowerPoint presentations for senior management. Participate in key planning meetings to solidify scope and identify resources.

- Document meeting minutes and track action items for Lab Testing Projects.

- Work with multiple clients and departments to gather data, schedule dates, and collect data requirements for scheduled projects.

- Create PowerPoint presentations for New Hires Welcome Packet.

- Use project databases to generate reports used for prioritization of Lab Test Projects.

Warner Bros	**Burbank, CA**	**6/2013–8/2013**

Senior Project Coordinator

- Managed Contractor Resource Program using spreadsheets and pivot tables for senior level management.

- Performed weekly analysis on contractor schedule variances.

- Provided the team with tracking issues and action items.

- Worked with senior leadership to gather requirements for scheduled projects.

- Provided visual testing for Fluster application for Executive Leadership.

- Developed Web instructions for Warner Bros. properties (Injustice, The CW App, and Flixter) specifically for Xbox 360.

- Developed Company newsletters to inform department of new technologies that impact Warner Bros. properties.

Wolcott Interiors and Architecture   Culver City, CA
1/2013 - 3/2013

Senior Project Coordinator

Managed 6 weekly financial status reports for senior level management using Excel spreadsheets.

■ Calendared meetings for prospective clients, architects and projects managers using Microsoft Outlook.

■ Created project contracts and work authorizations for senior project managers and executives. Produced meeting minutes and created action plans to track actions and issues.

■ Updated business organization charts using Visio and complied critical marketing correspondence.

■ Completed executive expense reports and distributed weekly project status reports to senior management.

■ Provided additional assignments and responsibilities as directed by supervisors. Also provided companywide announcements through telecom system.

TLS Talent Agency   Washington, D.C./N.C.
1/2012–12/2012

Executive Administrative Specialist

Resolve/discuss outstanding project issues and communicated work status to agents on a daily basis.

■ Developed proposals and completed high-level administrative projects.

■ Created PowerPoint presentations for senior management.

■ Submitted and managed casting information for clients.

■ Provided development notes and coverage on numerous scripts and treatments.

■ Assisted clients with confidential and human resource issues.

Kaiser Permanente,CCES Program   Rancho Cucamonga, CA
5/2010 - 11/2011

Senior Project Manager

■ Supervised a team of business analyst and consultants to develop business requirements and identify business artifacts.

■ Managed the day-to-day operational aspects of project Work Streams and scope, using Microsoft Project, Excel and Power-Point.

■ Produced project diagrams, timelines, and action logs using Visio and Excel.

■ All duties were leading to the completion of a software implementation deadline date for 8/2012.

AWARDS & RECOGNITION

■ Revenue Cycle PMO "Thank You Award" for the months: Sept., Oct., Nov., & Dec. 2009

■ Revenue Cycle PMO "You Rock Award" for the Year 2009

Appendix D

List of Jobs for Introverts

1. Social Media Manager
2. Actuary
3. Electrician
4. Political Scientist
5. Paralegal
6. Medical Records Technician
7. Graphic Designer
8. Technical Writer
9. Accountant
10. Computer Programmer
11. Truck Driver
12. Lab Technician
13. Market Research Analyst
14. Translator
15. Small Engine Mechanic
16. Forester
17. Museum Technician
18. Video Game Artist
19. Animal Care Worker
20. Petroleum Geologist

APPENDIX E

Job Description Matrix

Illustrated below is an example of a job description matrix. In Chapter 11, we discussed a job description matrix is a document that compares your skills and experiences with the qualifications, responsibilities, and requirements of a job descriptions. It can be used to quickly alleviate any doubt a future employer may have about your qualifications.

ABXY Corp	Candidate: Jared C. Powell
Open Position: IT Project Manager	
Education & Experience	
Min. 2 years of project management experience.	I have 7+ years of project management experience.
Associate's degree or equivalent from two-year college or technical school required, Bachelor's degree from four-year college or university preferred.	I have a B.S in Mechanical Engineering from Tuskegee University.
Excellent communication and customer relation skills.	As a project manager, communication skills are crucial when dealing with the daily project team and also dealing with stakeholders and/or the client. I have used my communication skills by providing crisp agendas and concrete status reports.

ABXY Corp	Candidate: Jared C. Powell
Open Position: IT Project Manager	
Ability to work with all levels of employees and produce results in a fast paced environment.	I believe a dynamic workplace is just a part of the job. In all of my jobs, I have been very comfortable in a fast paced environment, whether at ABXY Corp., DirecTV, or Farmer's Insurance.
Analytical mindset with attention to details.	I love to create spreadsheets, charts, presentations, and graphs.
Ability to handle confidential information.	Yes, whether its PCI or confidential job salary information.
Ability to work with minimal supervision. bilingual preferred.	As a project manager you have to be self-directed, independent and resourceful.
Other Qualifications	
Punctual and dependable attendance.	Yes, I am a professional project manager.
Free from alcohol and drug abuse.	Yes, I do not do drugs.
Understands the basic philosophy of ABXY Corp. and participates fully in carrying out its mission.	Yes, I am fully supportive of the ABXY Corp. mission statement. I truly believe in the message.
Adheres to ABXY Corp.'s values of Respect, Integrity, Service, & Excellence.	Yes, I am fully supportive of the ABXY Corp mission statement. I truly believe in the message.
Certificates, Licenses, Registrations	
Project Management Professional (PMP) Certification required.	Yes, I did pass the PMP.

ABXY Corp	Candidate: Jared C. Powell
Open Position: IT Project Manager	
English Language Skills	
Ability to read, analyze, and interpret general business periodicals, professional journals, technical procedures, or governmental regulations.	Yes, it was crucial I understood and was familiar with government regulations at Kaiser and at Farmer's Insurance as well as dealing with SOX controls and protecting PHI and PCI.
Ability to write reports, business correspondence, and procedure manuals.	I love to create spreadsheets, charts, presentations, and graphs and I did this at Kaiser Permanente
Ability to effectively present information and respond to questions from groups of managers, clients, customers, and the general public.	I love to create spreadsheets, charts, and give presentations to senior leadership and or the stakeholders. Provided both weekly and monthly status reports to all stakeholders on the CCES Program at Kaiser Permanente
Mathematical Skills	
Ability to calculate figures and amounts such as discounts, interest, commissions, proportions, percentages, area, circumference, and volume.	Can calculate figures and other amounts. I spent a lot of time solving math problems and learning new equations while studying for my degree in Mechanical Engineering. (Area of a triangle is 1/2 base*height)..

ABXY Corp	Candidate: Jared C. Powell
Open Position: IT Project Manager	
Ability to apply concepts of basic algebra and geometry.	Can calculate figures and other amounts. I spent a lot of time solving math problems and learning new equations while studying for my degree in Mechanical Engineering. (Area of a triangle is 1/2 base*height).
Reasoning Ability	
Ability to define problems, collect data, establish facts, and draw valid conclusions.	Yes, I have developed countless presentations and spreadsheets that consisted of data from various parties while at Kaiser Permanente
Ability to interpret an extensive variety of technical instructions in mathematical or diagram form and deal with several abstract and concrete variables.	Yes, I have a degree in Mechanical Engineering and have developed technical instructions and created mechanical drawing diagrams.
Computer Skills	
Must have advanced knowledge proficiency of computer programs in a Windows environment, including Word, Excel, Power Point, and E-mail.	Over 15 years of experience with the entire MS Office Suite (Word, PowerPoint, Excel, and Visio). Fluent with MS Outlook or Lotus Notes.
Contact Management systems	Familiar with Salesforce Integrations
Project Management software	MS Project and JIRA
Other software / systems	Sharepoint, Docushare, Remedy

ABXY Corp	Candidate: Jared C. Powell
Open Position: IT Project Manager	
Primary Responsibility / Summary	
The Project Manager is responsible for the planning, supervision, and management of large cross-functional enterprise projects with the goal of delivering project objectives on time and within budget.	Used the SDLC to develop multiple online insurance products: Graded Death Benefit and the 3 New Life products. Created the necessary deliverable documentation. Successfully delivered the Graded Death Benefit (GDB) and the 3 New Life Products to the Farmer's Digital Market Place and improved the online customer experience.
Essential Duties and Responsibilities	
Accountable for the definition, planning, scheduling, execution and successful completion of assigned projects. Use appropriate methodology to create work breakdown structures and to define all project phases, activities, tasks, and deliverables.	Used the SDLC to develop multiple online insurance products: Graded Death Benefit and the 3 New Life products. Created the necessary deliverable documentation. Successfully delivered the Graded Death Benefit (GDB) and the 3 New Life Products to the Farmers Digital Market Place and improved the online customer experience.

ABXY Corp	Candidate: Jared C. Powell
Open Position: IT Project Manager	
Coach, motivate, lead, and supervise project team while acting as a central point of communication for the team and stakeholders, including facilitating meetings and managing project expectations: influence team members to take positive action and accountability for the delivery of their assigned work.	Led a matrix project team of Quality Assurance (QA) testers, developers, and solutions consultants to implement functional and content level changes. Provided project schedules using MS Project and created/tracked change requests using Sharepoint. Scheduled weekly meetings to drive project forward and receive critical status updates.
Develop and manage key project artifacts and deliverables throughout the project lifecycle, including project charter, project plan, resource management plan, budget, dependency log, risk and issues log and shared project repository.	While at Kaiser Permanente I established project timelines for contract configurations, solidified project deliverables (Project Charter, Scope Document, Action Log, Risk Log), and obtained buy-in from stakeholders.
Conduct needs analysis producing requirement definition and functional specifications, garnering appropriate review and input from stakeholders.	While at Kaiser Permanente, I facilitated requirements defining sessions with key stakeholders in various departments. I established project timelines for contract configurations and obtained buy-in from stakeholders.
Ensure assigned projects are completed within estimated hours, schedule and budget.	While at Kaiser Permanente, I established project timelines for contract configurations, solidified project deliverables, and obtained buy-in from stakeholders

ABXY Corp	Candidate: Jared C. Powell
Open Position: IT Project Manager	
Actively engage stakeholders and communicate project status to the project team, Executive Sponsor, and IT Steering Committee.	Provided both weekly and monthly status updates to all stakeholders on the CCES Program at Kaiser Permanente. Presented a 20-page deck to CCES Senior Leadership during the claim system integration.
This position may require some travel (25% – 50%) a valid CA driver's license and state-required auto insurance is necessary. Driving records must be acceptable by Company's insurance vendor.	Yes, I have a valid driver's license. Driving record should not be a problem.

Appendix F

Thank You Letter Sample 1

Mxx Smith

Human Resources Director

ABXY Corp. Address

Date:

Dear Ms. Smith:

Thank you for taking the time to discuss the Project Manager position at ABXY Corp. with me on Thursday. The opportunity to work for a dynamic, fast-paced, innovative organization like ABXY Corp. is incredibly exciting. I am confident I will make an excellent fit as a Project Manager with ABXY Corp. because I am an achievement-oriented Project Manager with a proven reputation for effectively managing multiple projects on time and within budget.

As we discussed during our conversation, while at Kaiser Permanente I provided the executive leadership team with status reports and conveyed critical business objectives to key stakeholders. I also lead a team of QA testers, developers, and solutions consultants to complete various projects and deliver new functionality to the Digital Market Place.

I look forward to the opportunity to work at ABXY Corp. and exceed your expectations. Again, thank you for considering me for this exciting opportunity. I'm enclosing additional examples of my work product.

Thank you for your time and I look forward to hearing from you soon.

Sincerely,

Jared Powell

(xxx) xxx-xxxx

THANK YOU LETTER SAMPLE 2

Jared Powell

3308 Stone Ridge Avenue

Los Angeles, CA 90032

(310) 767- 7935

July 13, 2015

Marsha XXXX

Human Resources Director

AXSC Corporation

1303 Ventura Blvd Suite 320

Sherman Oaks, CA 91403 United States

Dear Ms. XXXX:

Thank you for taking the time to discuss the Project Manager position at AXSC Corporation with me on Thursday. The opportunity to work for a dynamic, fast-paced, innovative organization like AXSC Corporation is incredibly exciting. I am confident I will make an excellent fit as a Project Manager with your organization because I am an achievement-oriented project manager with a proven reputation for effectively directing multiple projects on time and within budget.

As we discussed during our conversation, while at Farmer's Insurance I provided the executive leadership team with status reports and conveyed critical business objectives to key stakeholders. I also lead a team of QA testers, developers, and solutions consultants to complete various projects and deliver new functionality to the Farmer's Digital Market Place.

I look forward to the opportunity to work at AXSC Corporation and exceed your expectations. Again, thank you for considering me for this exciting opportunity. I'm enclosing additional examples of my work product for your perusal.

Thank you for your time and I look forward to hearing from you soon.

Sincerely,

Jared Powell

(310) 766-7925

APPENDIX G

Examples of work to share for a Detailed Meeting Agenda.

Topic:	Work Stream Monthly Session
Date:	9/21/2012
Time:	10:00 am – 4:00 pm (Pacific)
Location:	Ontario, California - Ontario Hilton: Dolcetto Conference Room
Phone #:	**Call-in toll-free number (US/Canada):** 1-866-699-3239 **Access code:**575 844 926 **Meeting password:** Cces2010
Facilitator:	Jared Powell (Project Manager)
Purpose:	The purpose of the meeting/group is to formulate pricing policies and provide a framework for contract configuration and pricing alternatives. Working with our Contracting partners, we will develop a roadmap for the remediation of contracts that do not contain pricing methodologies currently managed within Xcelys. This remediation can consist of enhancements to Xcelys, codification or clarification of pricing terms, and/or an agreement to update the pricing terms as upon contract renewal. Additionally, we will identify best practices and drive process standardization.

Attendees: *(x indicates attendance)*		
☐ Joe Bob	☐ Peggy Sue	☐ Joe Smee
☐ John Doe	☐ Jane Doe	☐ Kelly Smith
☐ Jared Powell	☐ JP Stone	☐ Kevin Smith

Time	Agenda Item	Approx. Time Allocation	Facilitator
10:00 am 10:10 am	**Welcome & Introductions**	10 min	Jared Powell
10:10 am 10:30 am	**MO - Model Office** **Objective:** Review latest updates from Model Office (professional testing results, institutional contract configuration and go-forward approach for remaining configuration results)	20 min	John Doe
10:30 am 10:50 am	**Work Stream Report Out** **Objective:** To share status of activities in progress, including SBARs in queue, URDs, Demographic analysis, Post Model Office schedule and critical activities and deliverables over the next 30/60/90 days.	20 min	Jared Powell
10:50 am 11:20 am	**URD Status and Governance Process** **Objective:** To review final URDs submitted to Dell. Discuss Xcelys Governance structure and process, as reviewed with Xcelys executive leadership.	30 min	Jane Doe
11:20 am 11:50 am	**Provider Demographics** **Objective:** Review proposed approach to provider demographic analysis and clean-up, including timeline for completion.	30 min	Jane Doe
11:50 am 12:30 am	**SBAR: Allowed Greater than Billed** **Objective:** To review, identify any needed changes and discuss proposed recommendation(s).	40 min	JP Stone
12:30 pm 1:00 pm	**Lunch Break –** **Objective:** Gain a nutritious meal.	30 min	All

1:00 pm 1:30 pm	**SBAR: Visiting Member** **Objective:** To review, identify any needed changes and discuss proposed recommendation(s).	30 min	Janeti Doe
1:30 pm 2:30 pm	**Contract Sizing & Pay Method Analysis** **Objective:** Share analysis completed of contracts to identify opportunities for auto pricing upon Xcelys go-live.	1 hour	John Doe
2:30 pm 3:30 pm	**ICD-10 for the Contracting Work Stream**	1 hour	Joe Smee
3:30 pm 4:00 pm	**Next Steps & Wrap up** Review action items Review pending issues Discuss proposed agenda for October	30 min	Jared Powell

Date Opened	Action Items	Due Date	Status
7/19/2011	Incorporate stakeholder changes to the URDs - Business Consultants, Dell/Perot	8/16/2011	Open
7/19/2011	Outline solution approach options for getting external contracted provider demographics to support go-live, including how we get from current state to future state, including identification of data elements and gaps/missing elements –	7/29/2011	In progress
7/19/2011	Need to map OPVS fields to Xcelys and identify any gaps –	7/29/2011	Closed
7/19/2011	Current state business processes need to include KPIC and Self Funding – Annette Compton	7/22/2011	Open

7/19/2011	Share BPM Data Analysis Completed of Contract Terms and Auto/Non Auto Pricing	8/29/2011	In progress
7/19/2011	Need to review list of contract terms shared by Jerry/Data Elements Contracting needs in Xcelys -	8/12/2011	Closed
7/19/2011	Dental Contracts – Are Dental Claim forms (new state mandate) and appropriate Fee Schedules configured in Xcelys Model Office? Will they be before go-live? –	7/25/2011	In progress
7/19/2011	hare BPM Data Analysis Completed of Contract Terms and Auto/Non Auto Pricing – Jared Powell	8/13/2011	Open

ABOUT THE AUTHOR

Confessions of an Unemployed Professional is Jared Powell's first book. He holds a B.S. in Mechanical Engineering from Tuskegee University and received his PMP Project Management certification in 2009 and his Agile Expert Certificate in 2015. For over 14 years, Jared has worked in the Healthcare Field, Engineering and Construction Industry, the Solar Industry, and the Entertainment Industry. He is a Corporate Trainer and also the Executive Vice President of Books You Live By. Jared divides his time between Northern California and Southern California. He enjoys writing, lifting weights, playing soccer, and designing board games.

.

Made in the USA
San Bernardino, CA
14 January 2017